Learning from Comparative Public Policy

This textbook offers a fresh approach to the study of comparative politics and public policy. Instead of concentrating on why countries differ, *Learning from Comparative Public Policy* explores how countries can learn from each other about the success and failure of policy initiatives. With its theory and practice focus, the lively narrative analyses the cultural and resources problems involved in importing policies, and the roles of institutions, regulators, think tanks and experts. In addition to explaining the key tenets of policy analysis, the internationally renowned author offers a wide variety of international case studies and useful boxes to highlight examples. Invaluable reading for students of public policy, for policymakers and practitioners working in the public sector.

Key content includes:

– Learning from comparison;
– Defining a problem and creating awareness;
– Where to look for lessons;
– Applying the policy model;
– The problems of importing models;
– Using terms to evaluate future consequences.

Professor Richard Rose is Director of the Centre for the Study of Public Policy at the University of Strathclyde. He is a fellow of the British Academy and of the American Academy of Arts and Sciences. His writings have been translated into eighteen languages.

Learning from Comparative Public Policy

A practical guide

Richard Rose

Routledge
Taylor & Francis Group

LONDON AND NEW YORK

First published 2005
by Routledge
2 Park Square, Milton Park, Abingdon, Oxon OX14 4RN

Simultaneously published in the USA and Canada
by Routledge
270 Madison Ave, New York, NY 10016

Routledge is an imprint of the Taylor & Francis Group

Transferred to Digital Printing 2005

© 2005 Richard Rose

Typeset in Baskerville by
Keystroke, Jacaranda Lodge, Wolverhampton

British Library Cataloguing in Publication Data
A catalogue record for this book is available from the British Library

Library of Congress Cataloging in Publication Data
A catalog record for this book has been requested

ISBN 0–415–31741–X (hbk)
ISBN 0–415–31742–8 (pbk)

Dedicated to

All those who have the imagination and the mettle to search afar for knowledge.

Ein Mensch von mittelmäßigen Talent bleibt immer mittelmäßig, er mag reisen oder nicht – aber ein Mensch von superieuren Talent ... wird schlecht, wenn er immer in den nämlichen Ort bleibt.

Wolfgang Amadeus Mozart to his father, 1778

Contents

Boxed examples

Acknowledgements

In a very real sense this book reflects a lifetime of learning by the author. Growing up in a border state, Missouri, made me conscious of black and white differences in public policy. The Second World War and the postwar reconstruction of Europe showed that defeated nations could learn what not to do. In the course of a long professional career I have learned much through involvement with policymakers from Belfast and Brussels to Bogota and Beijing, and from working as a consultant for the World Bank, the OECD, the Council of Europe, and various non-governmental organizations, such as Freedom House and Transparency International.

Many discussions have occurred when no one knew what would happen next, that is, before the British Treasury accepted that it could not control the exchange rate of the pound, before Communist rulers accepted that their system was unsustainable, and before the gun came out again in Northern Ireland. Viewing history forward, when even the diagnosis of the problem is uncertain, makes me sympathetic to the difficulties of making decisions under conditions of uncertainty.

A book I wrote more than a decade ago, *Lesson-Drawing in Public Policy*, was a study in political science, providing a conceptual vocabulary for analyzing lesson-drawing. This book, instead, is a study in political engineering, that is, the application of social science knowledge to the world in which policymakers must make choices. It is not a book of explanation, for theories that specialize in explanation, such as rational choice, do not tell you how to do what is rational. This book is addressed to readers who want to learn how to draw lessons.

The immediate stimulus to write this book came from the Future Governance programme of the British Economic and Social Research Council. Its grant (L216252017) financed some of the time and effort required to think through this book. The programme director, Professor Edward C. Page, was constructively helpful in intellectual comments and in dealing with the bureaucracy of a programme grant. A stint as a specialist advisor to the British House of Commons Public Administration Committee study of targets for evaluating the performance of British policies provided a pointed reminder of the way in which many members of Parliament approach issues. Rather than joining Candide in celebrating the way in which decisions are often made, I prefer to follow Adlai Stevenson's epigraph for Eleanor Roosevelt: 'She would rather light a candle than curse the darkness.'

The author is far too experienced in the ways and waywardness of the world to think that any one country holds all the answers for other nations or that a single programme is best for all countries. One consequence of travel is that the comforts of home become more appealing. Knowledge of what other governments do is an antidote to unwarranted satisfaction. It is also a stimulus to take a fresh look at what is usually taken for granted at home. Although the difficulties of applying lessons are numerous, the costs of ignorance are substantial too.

Introduction

Why learn lessons from abroad?

> *It is always right for one who dwells in a well-ordered state to go forth on a voyage of enquiry by land and sea so as to confirm thereby such of his native laws as are rightly enacted and to amend any that are deficient.*
>
> Plato, *Laws*

The goal of this book is ambitious: it is to help readers deal with problems of public policy by drawing lessons from the experience of other governments. The object of looking abroad is not to copy but to learn under what circumstances and to what extent programmes effective elsewhere may also work here. Moreover, the failures of other governments offer lessons about what not to do at far less political cost than making the same mistakes yourself.

There is nothing novel in lesson-drawing. More than 2,300 years ago Aristotle studied the different ways in which Greek cities governed themselves in order to learn how to create the best political system. Having fought on the losing side in the Peloponnesian wars, Thucydides sought lessons about home-land security from the way in which disputes between nominal allies had led to defeat. The authors of the American constitution looked to Europe for lessons. Many of its most distinctive features reflected lessons about what not to do, learned from King George III's England. When Thomas Jefferson read Montesquieu he was doing so not to improve his French but in order to draw lessons that could be applied in writing the constitution of the United States.

This book is for readers who want to deal with problems in the real world of politics. It rejects the apolitical complaint of World Bank management consultants: 'The problem is not that one does not know what to do. The problem is that sociopolitical and bureaucratic obstacles in each country impede or block the implementation of good practices' (quoted in Olsen and Peters, 1996: 10). This book accepts that politics matters.

In a world in which people, money, and ideas increasingly move across national boundaries, this book challenges national policymakers to abandon the belief that the only wheel worth using is one that is invented at home. Policymakers can learn how improvements might be made by looking elsewhere. After all, that is how Japan turned from being a country that imported automobiles to being the world's biggest exporter of cars.

The need to learn

The first priority of a would-be policymaker is to learn what government is already doing. Learning the conventional wisdom of a government department involves 'learning how not to learn and how to live with the ignorance deemed appropriate' (Wenger, 1998: 40). As long as a programme produces satisfaction, there is no stimulus to learn. Public officials can concentrate on administering the status quo. The decision rule is simple: 'If it ain't broke, don't fix it.' A suggestion to look to a foreign country for new ideas can invite blank stares, puzzlement, or even an invitation to emigrate.

But the world does not stand still. When more people live long into old age, this causes frustrating queues for hospital treatment and pushes up public spending on health care and taxes. When automobile ownership expands, this increases traffic congestion, leading to dissatisfaction among motorists. The longer a policy is in place, the greater the risk that it becomes obsolete. Sooner or later, a programme that was once the solution to a difficulty itself becomes a problem. When things start going wrong, there is pressure on policymakers to come up with fresh measures to dispel dissatisfaction and media criticism, and opinion polls threaten the government of the day with unpopularity or even election defeat.

Policymakers do not seek fresh ideas for their own sake but to promote political satisfaction. Hence, the initial response to a demand for action is not to scan the world but to look within your own organization for a remedy. When under pressure, policymakers can look to their past experience for solutions that have worked before and try them again. Invoking a familiar remedy involves no learning and a minimum of change. But familiar remedies become obsolete too.

When past experience is no longer adequate, policymakers must start searching for a measure that works. At a minimum, a new programme can be said to work if it dispels dissatisfaction. Conscientious policymakers want more: they would also like to find programmes that will improve conditions in their society. This is not learning for its own sake; it is instrumental learning.

When action is demanded, individuals who offer fresh ideas are no longer disturbers of the peace but welcome. In such circumstances an economist may offer a proposal deduced with logical rigour from an abstract model of human behaviour. However, such a prescription is likely to be an oversimplification, leaving out the messy details that are the cause of the problem. A cautious policymaker can speculate aloud about an idea, asking, 'What would happen if we tried this?' The honest answer must be, 'We don't know.' The novelty of a speculative proposal is its chief drawback; there is no evidence of how it would work in practice.

Why foreigners?

The unique advantage of lesson-drawing is that its starting point is the observation of what is being done here and now. You can learn by observing a programme already in effect in another setting, rather than debating what might happen if an untried idea were adopted. This is consistent with the advice of Herbert Simon (1978), a political scientist with a Nobel prize in economics: 'The real world, in fact, is the most fertile of all sources of good research.' However, the horizons of policymakers differ greatly. Whereas diplomats routinely look abroad for ideas, and heads of Cabinet departments are concerned with national politics, local government officials may have their horizons confined by the boundaries of their county.

The maxim of the late Massachusetts Congressman Tip O'Neill, 'All politics is local', is familiar but misleading. Inasmuch as every member of Congress or Parliament is elected by a local constituency, it has a grain of truth. But when local problems are caused by national and international developments, the maxim distracts attention from where the action is. O'Neill himself recognized this, for instead of devoting his political life to his town council, he spent thirty-four years in Washington as a member of Congress.

In the twenty-first century it is the politics of the ostrich to claim that the problems of a single city or a single country are unique. The typical programmes of local government, such as education, sanitation, and fire protection, are common concerns of local governments everywhere in the world. Furthermore, many problems of major metropolitan areas cut across boundaries. For example, the New York metropolitan area covers parts of New Jersey and Connecticut too, and in the European Union economic problems of declining cities are common to more than a dozen different countries. While it is easiest for local policymakers to learn from friends and neighbours, if they share your ignorance, this is a reason to search further afield.

The programmes that are the distinctive responsibility of the national government, such as social security, managing the economy, and defence, have parallels in countries on every continent. In such circumstances, national policymakers can examine alternatives by looking abroad. For example, dozens of countries have national social security systems that differ in significant ways. Very few problems are unique to a single country, and those that are – for example, the United States' history of racial discrimination or continuing outbursts of political violence in Northern Ireland – are often unwanted parts of a country's past.

The distinction between national and international problems is increasingly blurred. Today, many problems of national government are *intermestic*, combining both international and domestic influences. While politicians remain responsible to a national electorate for economic conditions, these conditions are increasingly influenced by the movement of goods, services, and money across national borders. This is very evident among the twenty-five member states of the European Union (EU), and even more among the twelve EU countries that now have the euro as their common currency and interest rates set for them by the European Central Bank. Similarly, since Americans pay insufficient taxes to finance all the spending of the federal government, the current federal deficit relies on funding from Asian banks loaning money to the United States Treasury. When problems are intermestic, the success of a national programme depends not only on what national policymakers decide but also on what foreigners do. In such circumstances, national governments need to pay attention to what other countries do.

In a world in which money and people readily move across national borders, it is unrealistic to insist that nothing can be learned by looking abroad. Searching for lessons from foreign experience is possible because common problems do not produce identical responses. While all countries need to raise taxes, there are many different ways of doing so. This is illustrated by differences between American states in the rate of sales taxes and even more demonstrated by differences between the rates of value-added tax used throughout Europe and American sales taxes.

Differences in the responses that national governments make to a common problem offer the opportunity to compare the strengths and weaknesses of your own programmes with what other countries are doing. For example, the cost of health care met through tax revenue and through the private sector differs between countries, and so does the total sum spent. The British National Health Service is relatively cheap and publicly financed, while a relatively large part of American health care is privately financed and much more money is spent. However, crossnational differences in health programmes are not strongly correlated in modern societies with crossnational differences in health outcomes such as life expectancy.

Policymakers want to know not only how a programme works abroad but also: Could it work here? Therefore, this book faces in two directions. It is extroverted in emphasizing opportunities for learning from how other countries do things. The justification is clear: looking outwards offers policymakers fresh thoughts, whereas looking within your organization is likely to tell you what you already know or what you would like to forget. Yet the book is also introverted, since policymakers remain accountable to national electorates for what they do and don't do, and the purpose of learning what foreigners do is not to collect exotic information, but to draw practical lessons that can improve public policy at home.

Applying knowledge

The cast of people trying to influence government is vast. In the centre are politicians who decide whether or not a programme should be adopted. When making decisions, politicians are concerned with what will make them popular as well as with what works, and the two are often confused. Officials in the agencies dealing with a problem are experts in the substance and administration of programmes, and this is also true of involved interest group representatives. Opinion pollsters and media commentators help decide whether a programme is popular. While the citizens most affected by a programme can be numerous, their voice is often faint, for ordinary people are outside the loop within which decisions are made. However, citizens can be the ultimate arbiter of what is done when they vote for or against the government of the day. While not expecting busy policymakers to be reading this book today, I share the hope that some of you reading this book will be influencing decisions tomorrow.

Purpose of learning

Change in government is the subject of this book, but since organizations do not read books this volume is addressed to readers who are interested in learning not only to pass examinations, but also to understand how the vast storehouse of information in the literature of comparative politics can be used to improve public policy.

In one sense this book is Marxist, for Karl Marx immersed himself in books not only to understand the world but also to change it. However, the conclusions of lesson-drawing differ from Marxist prescriptions. Marxist-Leninist doctrines assume that a society can undergo a revolutionary transformation by the application of universal theories, and that the means of doing so is justified by the ends. By contrast, lesson-drawing is about learning in democratic political systems and it is sensitive to all the constraints that led to the failure of Marxist prescriptions that were forcibly applied in countries of Central and Eastern Europe.

Since readers differ in their political values, this book does not tell you what to think. It is designed to show you *how to think* about programmes dealing with familiar problems in unfamiliar places. It offers tools for understanding the way in which a foreign country deals with a problem that interests you. Even more importantly, it offers tools to translate foreign examples into a programme that can be applied at home.

Harried policymakers do not seek knowledge for its own sake; they engage in problem-oriented search, and the problem is often a fire in their in-tray:

> Problem-oriented search can be distinguished from both random curiosity and the search for understanding. It is distinguished from the former

because it has a goal and from the latter because it is interested in understanding only insofar as such understanding contributes to control. Such
search is engineering rather than pure science.

(Cyert and March, 1963: 121)

Lesson-drawing is an applied science, like engineering. Whereas theoretical
physics can discuss flight in terms of a series of equations, and applied physics
may use these equations to demonstrate on a computer how a plane could fly,
it is up to aeronautical engineers to build planes that do fly. Lesson-drawing
shares with civil engineering a concern with context, for a civil engineer would
not think of digging foundations for a bridge without first checking the soil and
the subsoil to verify how general principles can be adapted so that the bridge's
foundations will be sound in its particular context.

The application of knowledge to the world of practice is the purpose of
the professional schools of a university. Doctors, lawyers, and teachers do not
learn theory for its own sake but in order to deal with problems presented by
patients, clients, and unruly children. The pursuit of knowledge as a prelude to
action can also be found in classics of political science. Six hundred years ago
Niccolò Machiavelli set out general principles to guide the behaviour of the
prince of a very unruly Florentine republic. Confronted with regime change in
post-revolutionary France, Alexis de Tocqueville travelled to examine democracy in America, because, as he explained to his French readers, 'My wish has
been to find there instruction by which we may ourselves profit' (1954, 1: 14).

The subject of this book has much in common with the study of comparative
politics. Both start by rejecting methodological nationalism, the belief that you
can understand the politics of a country only by confining your study to what
happens within your country. Both also reject imperialist nationalism, that is,
the belief that you can understand the politics of every country by projecting
abroad what you know about your own country. Both lesson-drawing and comparative politics focus on differences between policies that national governments
adopt in response to a common problem. The primary concern of comparative
politics is to explain why countries differ in their policies; the explanations often
imply that these differences are persisting. Thus, an explanation is not a lesson,
because it offers no guidance about how positive achievements in one country's
programme can be used to improve policy in another country.

To draw a lesson properly, it is necessary to ask a series of questions about
how a programme works elsewhere in one or several countries. Since each
national government is responsible for hundreds of programmes, this book
cannot offer detailed information about all the programmes for which modern
governments are responsible. Such information can be found in textbooks and
scholarly monographs and increasingly on the World Wide Web. Because this
book is about how to analyse problems, a welter of detailed information would
also distract from the purpose at hand. Instead, the book uses boxes to highlight

basic principles of lesson-drawing. Footnotes to the vast literature of public policy are also kept to a minimum, for lesson-drawing is not about reviewing what other people have written but about learning to abstract knowledge from multiple sources of information.

With more than 175 recognized states in the world, there could be tens of thousands of links between a government seeking knowledge and a government with a programme worth knowing about. However, learning does not take place randomly; governments look to countries that they hope have something useful to offer. Among countries that belong to the Organisation for Economic Co-operation and Development (OECD), a group of the world's most modern societies, resources tend to be similar. In many developing countries, shortages of money, personnel, and administrative capacity are obstacles to adopting modern programmes. Yet money to introduce new programmes is available to poor countries through institutions such as the World Bank and national development agencies, and the money often comes with conditions that programmes be adopted that are drawn from the experience of rich countries donating the funds.

Among the countries of the world, the United States has a unique position. Not only is it populous, rich, and globally prominent, but also American universities now have more social scientists than in any other country. Yet claims of American uniqueness are profoundly ambiguous. Since Tocqueville's time, some scholars have viewed the United States as a vanguard nation, offering insights into future developments elsewhere. Presidents from Woodrow Wilson onwards have often sought to export American ideas of democracy to Europe and now the Middle East. However, some American scholars endorse theories of American exceptionalism (e.g. Lipset, 1996); this implies that its programmes cannot easily be exported to other countries. Yet systematic studies of the extent to which American public policies are comparable to those of other OECD countries are surprisingly few (but see Rose, 1974, 1991a; Wilson, 1998). Even rarer are books that argue that American exceptionalism is undesirable and Washington ought to import programmes from social democratic Europe (Kingdon, 1998; Walker and Wiseman, 2003).

Lesson-drawing rejects the idea of turning to a single country for lessons. No one government has a monopoly of wisdom, and differences between countries in political values mean that programmes advancing social democratic goals will be unattractive to free market governments and vice versa. More than that, lesson-drawing challenges the assumption that there is such a thing as American public policy or, for that matter, British, German, or French public policy. Within a country, programmes addressing different issues are likely to differ from each other more than programmes addressing the same problem in different countries. Thus, policy analysts searching for a new child care programme would turn not to colleagues in departments of transport or agriculture, but to comparable agencies in other countries.

Comparisons across national boundaries require a common language of discourse. Today, English is the language of comparative politics and the language most often spoken in intergovernmental organizations promoting policies. But this book is not just another look at the movement of ideas between London and Washington or Harvard and Oxford. Nor should it be, when public policies in twenty-three of the twenty-five countries of the European Union are administered in languages other than English. Readers who are not native English-speakers start with an advantage, for reading and thinking about public policy in two languages makes you sensitive to differences in the way that national governments handle common problems.

Next steps

The chapters that follow set out ten steps you need to take in order to determine whether or to what extent programmes in operation abroad could and should be applied at home (see Box Int.1). Of course, politicians in a hurry do not think systematically and often shortcut the process of analysis by jumping to a congenial conclusion supported by invoking a foreign country as a symbol of success. However, the consequence of leaping before thinking can be yet another policy failure.

The first step is to be clear about key concepts: what a programme is and is not, and what does and does not constitute a lesson. A programme is very different from a vague rhetorical invocation of policy goals. A programme specifies who does what, where and how, and at what cost. In lesson-drawing, the analysis of a foreign programme is an input to domestic policymaking. A lesson uses knowledge of foreign measures to create a programme that can be

---

Box Int.1   Ten steps in lesson-drawing

1 Learn the key concepts: what a programme is, and what a lesson is and is not.
2 Catch the attention of policymakers.
3 Scan alternatives and decide where to look for lessons.
4 Learn by going abroad.
5 Abstract from what you observe a generalized model of how a foreign programme works.
6 Turn the model into a lesson fitting your own national context.
7 Decide whether the lesson should be adopted.
8 Decide whether the lesson can be applied.
9 Simplify the means and ends of a lesson to increase its chances of success.
10 Evaluate a lesson's outcome prospectively and, if it is adopted, as it evolves over time.

applied at home or, in the case of learning from failure, a lesson shows how to avoid repeating foreign mistakes.

Catching the attention of policymakers is the second step in lesson-drawing, and it is not as easy as it sounds. As long as a programme appears to be producing satisfaction, busy policymakers will concentrate their attention on other measures for which they are responsible. However, when dissatisfaction arises there is pressure to do something – and programmes that produce political satisfaction elsewhere become interesting. Proponents of lessons from abroad can follow a two-pronged strategy, actively trying to generate dissatisfaction with the status quo and promising a better future if the lesson they offer is adopted.

A readiness to consider foreign ideas leaves open where you look. The third step in the search maps where lessons may be found. The simplest place to look is an organization's own history. However, lessons from the past are not helpful if its history is a record of failures. Where you look depends on where you start from. Geographical proximity encourages Canada to look to the United States; however, it does not make Britons look to Ireland or France. Psychological proximity is important too. British policymakers prefer to look across oceans to the United States or Australia. Political ties influence the direction of search too. The European Union draws together countries as dissimilar as Sweden, Spain, and Slovenia, yet the obligations of membership are an incentive to consider what other EU members do. Developing countries want to become as prosperous as developed countries: that can make them look to programmes of rich countries for ideas even though they lack the resources to finance them.

For a policy analyst, travelling abroad is not a holiday but the activity of an intellectual venture capitalist. It requires the investment of time, effort, and thought. Thanks to modern communications, there are now lots of facilities for planning a trip. Getting an accurate understanding of how a programme really works on the ground requires skills more akin to those of a journalist than to those of a scholar in a library or a civil servant. It is necessary to identify knowledgeable informants and ask questions that will collectively provide a rounded picture of how a programme operates – and what criticisms are made of it by those who are affected by it. The fourth step is becoming skilled in tricks of the trade that can be used to learn from foreigners.

Returning home raises new difficulties, for the excitement of seeing fresh faces is replaced by the challenge of convincing old opponents of change that a foreign programme could possibly work here. The next step is to create a cause-and-effect model of a programme. A model is the opposite of a case study full of anecdotes and thick with descriptive detail. It strips away the foreign-language terms that make a programme appear alien and concentrates on the essential elements in its operation. Removing the specifics of national context creates a portable model that can be used to develop a programme for application at home.

A lesson is not a photocopy of a foreign programme, nor is it a model devoid of national context. A lesson is created by 're-contextualizing' the generic model. This requires filling in details that are necessary but not integral to a programme, such as rules for employing its civil servants. Where national circumstances differ between the exporting and importing country, this sixth step introduces changes that vary from the original prototype – as long as this does not undermine its effectiveness. A lesson is more likely to be an adaptation or synthesis of programmes observed elsewhere. This is particularly the case in the European Union, where learning does take place, but does not lead to uniformity of programmes. The result of lesson-drawing is a proposal that is designed to fit into your country. While politicians may dismiss a foreign programme as fit only for foreigners, they cannot so easily ignore a lesson that could be applied within their own area of responsibility.

Whatever the origins of the programme, the next step is to respond to the question: should it be adopted? This question is about competing political values and interests; the latter often masquerade as the former. Technical advantages will be dismissed if a programme's goal – for example, the redistribution of income – is in conflict with the dominant values of the government of the day. Government decisions are not made by a single-minded leader but by coalitions of organizations with diverse values and interests. Thus, the veto of a lesson on the grounds of political unacceptability is a stumbling block, but it need not be a permanent obstacle. Even if all major parties reject a lesson, it can remain a policy option, to be invoked as and when political values and interests alter.

If a lesson is politically acceptable, the eighth step is to decide: can a lesson be applied? How much money does it require? What sorts of personnel are needed to administer it? In OECD countries, resources are usually not an absolute barrier to adopting a lesson. A greater obstacle is likely to be the wicked context problem, that is, fitting a new measure into a crowded field of policy in which inherited programmes are maintained by the force of political inertia. In developing countries, by contrast, shortages of personnel and money are often major barriers to applying lessons. Furthermore, cultural misunderstandings are much more likely, because foreign aid staff may offer recommendations that are a projection of their own culture and that, taken out of that context, will fail if applied uncritically.

The success of any new programme is contingent – it may or may not produce political satisfaction – and the greater novelty of lessons from abroad makes risks greater than new proposals based on domestic experience. The ninth step is to think of things that can be done to increase the likelihood of success. A programme that has a clearly defined objective, a single goal, and a simple design with few essential elements is much more likely to succeed than a programme with vague purposes, multiple goals, and complex mechanisms for producing benefits. If possible, a lesson should make use of tested social and technical procedures and be flexible as to means. Because a lesson has foreign associations, the range of symbols that can be manipulated to win support for it or mobilize opposition to it is much greater than for a conventional domestic measure.

Policymakers are more interested in the future than the past. Because the future is unknown, promoters of new programmes can speculate enthusiastically about its benefits and ignore undesirable consequences. A major advantage of drawing a lesson from abroad is that foreign evidence can be used to put bounds on speculation. The adoption of a lesson is not the end of the learning process. Once introduced, a lesson will evolve. It generates feedback that can signal the need to adapt it to deal with problems that were not initially anticipated. If the response generates political satisfaction, then as time goes by what was once a lesson from abroad will become an established commitment of your national government.

Stage I
Getting started

Step 1

Understanding programmes and lessons

A wise person's question is half the answer.
Old proverb

Policymakers live in a world rich in information. A Google search for 'traffic congestion' identifies more than half a million web site references about traffic problems in places as far apart as Atlanta, Athens, and Beijing. A super-abundance of information creates a problem of selection. If you lack the ability to extract knowledge from a flood of details, you will be drowned in detail. The art of lesson-drawing (for it is a creative activity as well as a science) is to under-stand which features of a foreign programme are essential and which are not.

You need concepts to guide the selection of information relevant for lesson-drawing from books and from the ever-expanding World Wide Web. As a Nobel laureate in physics has emphasized:

> Science depends on concepts. These are the ideas which receive names. They determine the questions one asks, and the answers one gets. They are more fundamental than the theories which are stated in terms of them.
>
> (Thompson, 1961: 4)

Concepts are absolutely essential in order to draw lessons across national boundaries, for concepts provide the common vocabulary with which to relate features of a programme that operates in Dutch or French to a lesson to be applied in an English-speaking land. Concentrating on concepts avoids the problems that arise when foreign words make phenomena that are conceptually the same appear different or, alternatively, when the same word is a label for practices that in actuality are different.

Policy is an inadequate word to use in lesson-drawing because it has multiple meanings. It can refer to any topic that is a concern of government, such as foreign policy or economic policy; this usage leaves vague what, if anything, government is doing to deal with that concern. Policy can also refer to the intentions of politicians. An election campaign pledge to introduce a full-employment policy does not specify the means by which this goal is to be achieved. Third, policy can refer to the programmes that government uses to realize the policy intentions that politicians declare.

Programmes are the stock in trade of policy analysis. A programme is a specific measure that sets out the way in which public employees are authorized to spend money in pursuit of stated objectives. A programme is about the 'how' of public policy. In the absence of a programme detailing the nuts-and-bolts means by which good intentions are to be achieved, a statement of good intentions may produce a 'feel-good' effect, but the same can be said of a blast of hot air on a cold morning. To succeed as a policymaker, you must be good at designing a programme as well as at winning the political support necessary to adopt and maintain it.

A *lesson* is the outcome of learning; it specifies a programme drawing on knowledge of programmes in other countries dealing with much the same problem. A lesson is very different from a proposal to alter an existing programme, because it is about introducing something new. Yet a lesson has an empirical base, for it makes use of observation and evidence of a measure currently in effect elsewhere. A lesson does more than simply endorse what another government does. It adapts what is done elsewhere into a programme that can be applied by government at home.

Lesson-drawing has a lot in common with the practice of medicine. Both doctors of medicine and masters of public policy require theoretical and practical knowledge to deal with the problems that regularly confront them. The first step is diagnosing the cause of a problem. The purpose of diagnosis is not just to explain but also to prescribe an intervention that will improve conditions. In a hospital emergency room as in a political debate, pathological symptoms can be palpable, but their cause is not always clear and there can be uncertainties about what to prescribe. Any prescription drawn from foreign experience must be hedged with qualifications about success. Likewise, doctors shy away from promising that their treatment will be successful for, even if intervening in the human body is less unpredictable than in the body politic, the outcome is far from certain. Medical journals, like social science journals, regularly contain articles documenting the extent to which experimental interventions have not met desired goals.

A policy analyst's tool kit must have both general-purpose tools for designing programmes and specialist instruments relevant to a particular problem at hand. This chapter concentrates on two basic concepts of comparative public policy: understanding what a programme is and understanding what a lesson is and is not. Developing skill in using these tools does not guarantee success, but without them you are vulnerable to swallowing at face value the buzz words and hype of globetrotting policy entrepreneurs.

Programmes as building blocks

Programmes are the stuff of public policy; they are concrete measures for doing such things as delivering hospital care; regulating trading on the stock market; or maintaining the safety of airline passengers. Programmes organize and direct major resources of government – laws, money, personnel, and organizations – towards identifiable ends. The goals of programmes vary. Some goals target individuals, such as recipients of social security payments or children with specific physical disabilities. Others are addressed to organizations, whether in the public sector, such as local authorities or the police, or the private sector, such as firms emitting high levels of pollutants; or to conditions that concern both sectors, such as health and safety at work. Immigration programmes affect foreign citizens, and defence programmes are directed at unfriendly foreign states.

Programmes combine the 'hardware' and the 'software' needed to advance towards a policy goal (cf. Rogers, 1995: 12). The hardware consists of laws, money, personnel, and other organizational resources that are necessary to launch a new programme. However, they are insufficient to put a programme into effect. Software is also required, including the training of officials in new tasks, the development of informal procedures for integrating a new programme into existing public institutions, and delivery systems linking public agencies with intended beneficiaries.

Every programme is a mixture of resources, and the mix varies from programme to programme. Paying pensions is money-intensive; regulating companies is law-intensive; providing child care is labour-intensive; and health care is both labour- and money-intensive, since doctors, nurses, and hospital staff are required in large numbers, and all must be paid (Rose, 1985).

Programmes are the tangible embodiment of policy commitments. Their basis in law makes them as permanent as the statute book as well as fundamentally different from the transitory pledge of a politician during an election campaign. A law remains in effect until it is repealed, and repeal happens relatively rarely. A law binds public officials to organize activities to deliver benefits under specified rules applicable to everyone who is entitled to claim a benefit. In turn, this creates popular expectations that the programme will work, that is, deliver the benefits to which people are entitled. A programme commitment is the firmest commitment that a government can make to achieve a policy intention. This remains the case even if success is frustrated by events outside the control of government, such as a downturn in the international economy.

From the administrative perspective of a government department, a programme works if its inputs of resources are effectively transformed into outputs delivered to those lawfully entitled to receive them. For example, a programme intended to help unemployed youths can be said to work if most eligible youths participate in the programme and manage to get a job afterwards. From the perspective of an elected officeholder, a programme works if it produces political satisfaction. Searchers for lessons from abroad seek programmes that work in both the administrative and the political sense.

Across a government's range of public policies, there are big differences between programmes. For example, programmes for national parks have little in common with education programmes, and neither has much in common with defence measures. A study of British government programmes to regulate risk found 'striking differences in programmes between one domain of risk and another within a single state' (Hood *et al.*, 2001: 5).

A fundamental reason for looking to other nations for lessons is that differences between programmes within a country are often greater than those between programmes addressing the same problem in different countries. For example, programmes to supply clean water to cities in different OECD countries have more in common than do any one government's programmes to train primary school teachers and to supply clean water. In such circumstances, it makes sense for national policymakers responsible, for example, for a programme for clean water to look to counterparts in other countries. Moreover, since national governments respond to a common problem in different ways, learning about these differences can constitute useful knowledge.

Parallel and interdependent programmes

The programmes of a national government can be unique to one country, operate in parallel with many countries, or be functionally interdependent on what happens outside national boundaries.

Lesson-drawing is possible only if policymakers in different governments face a common problem. While every government programme has a different history, this does not make it inimitable. Unique programmes are exceptional and often not desired. For example, the institutional procedures for deciding the outcome of the American presidential election of 2000 are without parallel in other countries. The only lessons that other national governments want to learn from that event are how to avoid the 'hanging chads' problem of Florida and achieve a definitive election result without the conflict between courts evident in deciding the Florida count.

Parallel programmes

When many governments deal with a similar problem, their efforts are parallel if the activities of each remain as separate as the jurisdictions of different national governments. For example, while the United States and Britain each have a social security programme, the former pays benefits to people who have been employed in the United States and the latter to British workers. The important analytic point about parallel programmes is that they are comparable. Since authorities usually respond to a common problem differently, there is an opportunity to learn positive and negative lessons by comparing how parallel programmes differ.

Taxation is a field with many parallel programmes, for every government must raise revenue to finance its activities, and they do so by imposing a repertoire of income, corporation, sales and excise, and other taxes. Each tax is paralleled by taxes in up to a hundred or more other countries. Thus the way in which one country levies an income tax or a corporation tax can be compared with the way in which others do so. The internationalization of economic activity has given national governments and multinational corporations incentives to pay attention to the tax laws of other countries and the internationalization of economic education creates a transnational community of tax experts; and international institutions such as the International Monetary Fund and the Organisation for Economic Co-operation and Development routinely disseminate examples of tax measures that they consider best practice.

To describe parallel programmes as converging is a mistake. Even if parallel programmes become similar in their design, they do not unite into a single programme that is the same for people in different countries. Moreover, empirical research demonstrates that theories about economic pressures forcing programme convergence are mistaken, for they ignore the capacity of national governments to maintain national differences in the face of crossnational pressures.

Where you look for parallels depends on the level of government faced with a problem. When a problem arises in local government, parallels can be found with neighbouring authorities in the same county, region, or country. Providing parks and recreation is a typical example of such a highly decentralized service. If there is a problem, the local director of leisure services can look for lessons to parallel departments in the same metropolitan area, county, or state, or elsewhere in the country. In a centralized system, educational standards and a substantial portion of educational finance are the responsibility of the national government. It can then use its supervisory powers to monitor the performance of local authorities and try to promote lesson-drawing between the most and least successful school districts that it oversees.

A programme that is the sole responsibility of central government is uniform nationwide, for example, social security. A uniform national programme guarantees territorial justice, that is, equal treatment of citizens wherever they live in the country. Moreover, in an era in which there is substantial population mobility, a national programme guarantees that people who move within a country retain their rights to the same social security benefits. For this to happen, social security taxes must be collected nationally. When there is a single national programme, people searching for lessons about social security programmes or about taxation must turn to foreign countries.

Interdependent programmes

A programme is interdependent when what is done by one government is influenced by what is done by other governments. International trade is a classic example of interdependence, for a country's exports depend on the extent to which other countries are prepared to import what it produces. When there are interdependencies between the programmes of different governments, national policymakers must pay attention to what is done elsewhere, or risk failure. While a state can still make laws applying within its own jurisdiction, when there are interdependencies the effect of its laws will depend on what is done by other countries.

Interdependence requires an awareness of crossnational differences. For example, in continental Europe motorists drive on the right while in Britain and Ireland national laws require driving on the left. Thus, on opposite sides of the English Channel, official road signs warn drivers in English and French to remember which side of the road to drive on.

Interdependence does not require programmes to be uniform. Differences in national resources make sure this is not the case: for example, the small states of Eastern Europe that have joined NATO share a common goal with the United States, but Estonia and Slovenia cannot pretend to duplicate American military force. In international trade, small countries attempt not to copy the manufacturing programmes of large countries but to export niche products: Denmark, for example, has traditionally specialized in exporting dairy and pork products, while Liechtenstein has specialized in very private banking.

A variety of national programmes are necessarily interdependent. Defence programmes depend on what potential enemies may do. American military thinking has been doubly transformed in the past two decades by the collapse of the Soviet Union and by transnational terrorism. Environmental issues are another area of interdependence, for the effectiveness of, for example, local clean air acts is affected by winds blowing polluted air from factories in other parts of the same metropolitan area; Canadian clean air programmes depend on the effect on pollution of American programmes, and in Europe governments trying to clean up the Rhine and the Danube rivers depend on what is done by national governments upstream.

Since the linkages of interdependence often differ from those set out in national constitutions, sovereignty is now variable (Jönsson *et al.*, 2000: 72ff.). The trade in toys is an example, linking small-town retailers in Japan with multi-national corporations in the United States (Box 1.1). Many programmes that appear independent become interdependent when they interact with similar programmes in other jurisdictions. The sprawling character of large metro-politan areas can turn local road programmes into inter-state problems; for example, the Beltway that carries traffic around Washington, DC, runs through Maryland and Virginia. In England, the scale and sprawl of the greater London

Box 1.1 International interdependence in toy markets

Traditionally, toys were made of wood or cloth within the household by parents or by children themselves. While in poor countries households may still make their own toys, with economic development the manufacture of toys became an industry. Within a country, national manufacturers produced toys and games for a national market and sale through locally based retailers. A few specialist toys were exported within Europe at a premium price.

By the middle of the twentieth century, low-wage countries in Asia began to use cheap labour to produce cheap toys for export to mass markets in the United States. Today, much of the stock of toy shops in the most prosperous countries is imported from third-world countries where low wages allow for the cheap production of these labour-intensive goods. Expensive electronic toys have been developed in Japan, marketed internationally, and produced wherever it was cheapest. In addition, some toys have been branded by multinational corporations such as Disney Productions, and marketed worldwide.

The growth of multinational retailing has added a new level of interdependence, as local retailers and multinational chains compete in the same market. In a trip to Tokyo, the forty-first president, George Bush, talked about toys as well as high policy, complaining that Japanese legislation protecting small retail toy shops violated on international treaty commitment to free trade because it inhibited the development of chain stores such as the American retailer Toys R Us in Japan.

area makes its traffic a national problem, and the opening of the Channel Tunnel to France has added an international dimension to traffic problems.

At the end of the Second World War, national governments took responsibility for promoting economic growth and avoiding the unemployment that had dogged all continents during the 1930s. National policymakers assumed that they had the power to achieve these goals, if only they could identify the programmes to do so. For a quarter-century most governments appeared to be succeeding. The growth in national economies was accompanied by growth in international trade and the liberalization of currency exchange, so that dollars and pounds could be traded in foreign markets while national policymakers slept. The result was the internationalization of national economies. The oil price shocks of the 1970s offer public and expensive evidence of economic interdependence. In response, the leaders of the world's seven major economies began holding annual G7 (later G8) summit meetings to discuss how to relate their national economic programmes to international economic activities.

The recognition of interdependence creates an incentive for national governments to create institutions to co-ordinate their national programmes. When newly established national postal services found that they were being asked to send and deliver letters to foreign countries, they founded the Universal Postal Union in 1874 to establish procedures for handling mail across national boundaries. Today the organization has 189 member countries.

The European Union is a prime example the importance of the creation of institutions in response to an awareness of interdependence. It originated when French and German leaders reckoned after the Second World War that integrating two industries critical for war production – coal and steel – would make a third world war impossible. The adoption of the Single Europe Market Act a generation later was another major increase in interdependence through the reduction of trade barriers within Europe. It has broadened the powers of the European Commission to discourage national programmes that favour citizens of one country and to promote programmes intended to make virtually the whole of Europe into a single national market.

What a lesson is – and is not

When I started writing about lesson-drawing more than a decade ago (Rose, 1991b, 1993), references to 'lessons' were usually casual; the term was never defined. When the term is used today, its meaning is often abused. In a world of television sound bites, politicians shoot from the lip and draw lessons without thinking. Likewise, the lessons that one politician draws from his or her personal experience cannot be projected on to every citizen, let alone on to governments in other societies on other continents.

The distinctiveness of lessons

A lesson is a distinctive type of programme, because it draws on foreign experience to propose a programme that can deal with a problem confronting national policymakers in their home environment. Because a lesson is created by extracting knowledge from the experience of other countries, it differs from the normal practice of learning from your own experience.

A lesson is much more complex than a simple exhortation to 'be like America' or 'be like Japan'. It is a practical, nuts-and-bolts outline of the means as well as the ends of policy. It identifies the laws, appropriations, and personnel and organizational requirements needed for a programme to be put into effect. Lessons are thus much more than a politician's prescription of goals and priorities, such as fighting inflation or helping the poor. Such statements are inadequate to guide action because they are vague about the means that can be used to put these principles into effect. In the absence of details about how to get there from here, the prescribed goals are not lessons that can be applied. At most, they can be used to decide whether or not a proposed lesson is politically acceptable (see Step 7).

A lesson omits information that is interesting but non-essential and includes what is essential to make a programme work. It thus contains far fewer details than a case study of how a foreign programme operates. The narrative character of a case study encourages the inclusion of thick prose descriptions of the personalities of leading programme officials and of colourful incidents that can lighten discussion of administrative structures. However, such details are often not essential to the operation of a foreign programme and, in any event, are irrelevant to any lesson that may be drawn from it for application elsewhere. The information in a case study is only the starting point of learning; the end point is drawing a lesson that uses such knowledge to propose a programme to achieve similar effects (or avoid a similar disaster) in another country.

Like diffusion studies of the sequential adoption of measures in response to a common stimulus (for example, the spread of anti-smoking legislation or of Internet use), lesson-drawing is about the introduction of parallel programmes in more than one country. However, the focus of diffusion studies is on the sequence in which different local, state, or national governments respond to a common stimulus, such as the need of retired people for an income in old age. Thus, diffusion studies are concerned with the timing of adoption of national social security legislation and with the relationship between countries that are early adopters and late adopters (Rogers, 1995). Diffusion studies are more concerned with when a response is made rather than what is done. By contrast, the focus of lesson-drawing is on the programmes that are adopted in the process of diffusion. Since national governments will differ to a greater or lesser degree in how they respond, this provides opportunities for learning from the experience of others. However, lesson-drawing does not share the deterministic assumption of diffusion studies that all countries will sooner or later adopt a more or less similar programme in response to a common stimulus.

Lesson-drawing expands the scope for choice in the national political agenda, for it adds to proposals generated by domestic experience the stimulus of examples drawn from foreign experience. It does so without a commitment to a particular set of partisan values. The only condition for its use is that exponents of a value can locate an example of a programme already in effect elsewhere, a qualification that rules out Utopian programmes. It is up to policymakers to decide where to look for programmes that they might emulate. When a social problem arises, policymakers with different ideological outlooks can turn to different countries in search of lessons. Pro-market governments are likely to avoid Scandinavia, while social democratic governments are much more likely to head north in search of lessons consistent with their values.

Lesson-drawing accepts the contingency of public policy. Because it specifies the conditions that must be met for a programme to be effective, it can also identify under what circumstances a programme that works in one country will *not* work in another. It thus avoids the one-size-fits-all prescriptions of international management consultants and foreign aid advisors who recommend the same programme as the best without regard to national context. It also avoids the bias inherent in analyses of policy transfer, since that term focuses attention on programmes that can or could be imported from abroad at the expense of giving attention to the obstacles to applying lessons at home. Whereas a computer manufactured in Asia will work the same in the United States and in Europe, a programme in effect in Sweden will not necessarily be adaptable for application in Japan, and even less so in China. Even though programmes are not as portable as a laptop computer, this does not mean that there is a total blockage on applying lessons from abroad. The analytic question is: under what circumstances and to what extent can a programme that works there provide a lesson that can be applied here?

A lesson can be a warning about what not to do, and the value of avoiding mistakes is as great as the potential gains from positive lessons. More than that, a lesson can explain why a programme has failed by analysing what went wrong in detail in order to see whether failure was due to insufficient resources, political opposition, administrative difficulties, an unwillingness of citizens to cooperate, or a basic flaw in the logic of a programme. If resource limitations are the cause of failure, this implies that a programme could work in a country that dedicated sufficient money and personnel to its implementation. However, if failure is due to a programme having contradictory goals, this is a clear warning about what not to do.

A lesson is a bridge across time as well as space. It combines knowledge about what is happening in another country today with a specific proposal about actions that a government here might take to improve public policy in future. Because a lesson is future-oriented, it cannot be evaluated empirically; however, it is possible to evaluate empirically programmes in other countries that have served as its template.

What a lesson is not

Politicians are fond of rhetorical lesson-drawing, that is, citing examples from foreign countries to 'prove' that what they want to do is right – or to trash what their opponents are proposing. An American politician can invoke negative stories about the treatment of patients in the British health service as an argument against socialized medicine, while a British politician can invoke negative stories about the exclusion of tens of millions of Americans from health insurance as an argument against the market provision of medical care.

A television documentary about how a foreign government copes with a problem can stir up popular interest in a national problem and suggest what *might* be done about it. But television is very selective in what it can communicate: it is far better at showing personalities, who cannot move between political systems, than at describing the complex methods used to calculate unemployment benefit. Therefore, the prescription that a television documentary can offer will, at best, provide only the sketchiest of information about how a foreign example could be translated here.

The potential number of 'lessons' that can be drawn from history is almost infinite if the past of every country from China to Canada can be searched for examples. It remains very great if attention is simply focused on a restricted area of public policy such as social security or education in two dozen or more European Union or OECD countries. The problem with drawing lessons from history is that there is so much of it. While an academic social scientist might use the expanse of history to undertake systematic statistical analysis, policy-makers prefer to draw conclusions from familiar examples rather than from multivariate statistics. The choice – for example, in foreign policy between diplomatic negotiation or military action – is thus more likely to reflect the goals of those invoking history to justify their actions than a careful systematic analysis of past and present (see Step 3).

Officials of international organizations can draw on their prestige and financial resources to offer prescriptions masquerading as lessons from experience. After the fall of the Berlin Wall in 1989, international agencies poured large quantities of personnel, advice, and money into post-Communist countries. After a decade, the World Bank commissioned a report with the stated purpose of identifying 'lessons for Eastern Europe and the former Soviet Union'. The chief 'lessons' offered were:

- Encourage the creation of new firms.
- Impose financial discipline on loss-making firms.
- Strengthen legal and regulatory controls of private sector and state-owned enterprises.
- Avoid early beneficiaries of privatization capturing the state and blocking further reforms.

However justifiable these recommendations may appear to their authors, they are not lessons, for they lack the programmatic details showing how new firms can be created, legal institutions created and laws enforced, and powerful domestic financial interests overcome. Such statements are no more and no less than prescriptions about what ought to be done (World Bank, 2002: ix–x, xxviii–xxix).

The 'lessons' of rational choice analysis suffer the opposite defect: they are not based on any actual country or historical event. The starting point for rational choice analysis is the creation of an abstract and closed social system with a limited number of explicit assumptions about how politicians are expected to behave. There are no references to the specific circumstances of any country. The abstract nature of the model makes cause-and-effect relationships crystal clear, and deductions can be made with the logical rigour of pure mathematics. The 'rational' conclusion is thus an example drawn not from real life but from a radically simplified and abstract world. The great difficulty with rational choice analysis is not the application of knowledge from one real country to another, but the translation of its prescriptions from the world of pure theory to the messy context of a real country. Up to a point, economists have recognized the need to complement complex deductive models or inductive statistical analyses by citing stylized facts in the form of stories that are, in the literal sense, fables. However, doing so risks 'substituting dogma for measurement' (Black, 1997: 450).

Big ideas that circulate across international boundaries can and do influence the way in which policymakers think about the problems confronting them. For example, for a quarter-century after the Second World War the ideas of John Maynard Keynes influenced more than a generation of policymakers wanting to promote economic growth and keep a low level of unemployment. However, in the 1970s worldwide inflation became the priority concern of economic policymakers, and the monetarist ideas of Milton Friedman gained international dominance. Both sets of ideas were broad enough to attract interest across continents as well as national boundaries. But both suffered the defect of being 'too big'. While the thrust of their analysis was clear enough to rule out many programmes, it remained sufficiently open that many different, and sometimes conflicting, programmes could be justified as consistent with Keynesian or Friedmanite principles. In Cambridge, England, Keynes's intellectual home, there was the saying, 'Whenever five economists get together, there are always six opinions – and two of them belong to Keynes.' Similarly, policymakers attempting to apply Friedman's monetarist ideas in their national setting have been confronted with differences of opinion about whether the supply of money in their country should be measured by M1, M2, or M3 – or whether there is any satisfactory empirical measure that they can target to secure desired effects.

To learn a lesson, policymakers must travel further than the nearest coffee machine in search of ideas. Examining programmes that deal with familiar problems in an unfamiliar setting forces policymakers to step outside their everyday routine and learn by a process that is aptly described as 'distancing' (Argyris, 1982).

Step 2
Creating awareness of problems

*Public problems are not just out there waiting to be dealt with. **Policymaking** is not simply problem-solving. It is also a matter of setting up and defining problems in the first place.*

Charles Anderson, 'The Logic of Public Problems'

Politicians like to be associated with success. As long as almost everyone concerned with a programme is satisfied, the diagnosis is simple: no problem. In such circumstances there is no need to think about changing the programme and even less to seek lessons from abroad. A programme does not have to be internationally outstanding to produce contentment; it is sufficient for it to be considered 'good enough'.

Policymakers tend to judge the future by the past. The government of the day inherits many programmes from its predecessors. Inherited programmes run by routine; they are carried forward by the force of political inertia. The laws that govern most public programmes were enacted by politicians who left office a long time ago; they are delivered by public employees trained decades ago; and the politics of budgeting results in this year's expenditure being much the same as that of the year before (Rose and Davies, 1994). If those who benefit from a programme – whether as recipients or as public employees – regard it as satisfactory, today's governors can take credit for a measure introduced well before they won office or even before they were born.

Routines are the tramlines of public policy; they set out the path that officials follow in their daily round of delivering public services. Bureaucratic routines enable lower-level public employees to administer programmes without troubling policymakers nominally responsible for what they do. At the top of government, policymakers must hoard their time and manage by exception: only if the bulk of the programmes run by routine do they have time to do what is urgent and of highest political priority. When a leading official describes a programme as satisfactory, it usually means that everything appeared all right when he or she last looked.

The longer a programme has been in place, the more likely it is to creak and squeak, because of changes in society and in the demands of its recipients. Government lacks the discipline of 'bottom-line' indicators of success or failure that profitmaking companies have. Businessmen who brush aside evidence of falling sales or rising costs risk going out of business. By contrast, many public agencies are monopoly suppliers of programmes and rely on tax revenues to pay for whatever they deliver. When signs of dissatisfaction start to appear, policymakers can ignore complaints in the hope that they will go away, or they can defend the status quo. The incentives for a policymaker to do nothing are strong if a prospective difficulty will become serious only after he or she leaves office.

If discontent leads to public awareness of a problem, the immediate response of policymakers is to try to keep it within the loop, that is, to diagnose the problem in familiar terms and to ask familiar faces to apply a familiar remedy that has delivered satisfaction previously. If minor amendments can be made to reduce complaints, this can be trumpeted as a major achievement. Keeping action within the loop minimizes effort and is comforting to policymakers. But it may not be reassuring to those on the receiving end of a programme.

When dissatisfaction rises, inaction invites criticism of a 'do-nothing' government. This is good news for policy entrepreneurs, because it creates a demand for a novel programme to still complaints. Academic experts and pressure groups can prescribe novel measures that may be based on lessons from abroad. Even if a programme appears satisfactory to most people, the opposition party can try to generate discontent by looking for scandals in the administration of programmes. If no scandals can be found, it can assert that a programme is not good enough and promise to make it better still if it wins the next election.

This chapter examines different facets of awareness. The simplest situation is that in which the public is satisfied and policymakers do not have any need to do anything, except take credit for what is running by routine. However, sooner or later unexpected events can stimulate a rise in dissatisfaction, forcing policymakers into action. In an increasingly cosmopolitan policy environment, the publication of international comparisons can also stimulate dissatisfaction, if a country's programme does not appear to be up to international standards. This encourages policy entrepreneurs to offer a best-practice solution, but such programmes often have limited applicability outside their country of origin. However, the process of international benchmarking not only creates an awareness that a national government could do better, it also calls attention to a wide range of programmes abroad that appear to produce better results.

No problem; we're satisfied

As long as there is satisfaction with the status quo, there will be little demand from policymakers for information about what other countries are doing, for it is politically and economically inefficient to risk disrupting the status quo by encouraging evaluation from outside the loop. Policymakers can reckon a programme is satisfactory if there is positive evidence that it is successful or an absence of criticism to disturb their complacency. If criticisms are voiced, policymakers can claim that a programme is good enough or that, whatever the problem was yesterday, a new government measure now has the problem under control.

Evidence

The activities of an established programme routinely generate evidence about its administration. Statistics show how much money is being spent and how many people are employed, how many claims are being made for benefits or how many are being made to feel the brunt of regulations, and how quickly or slowly officials act in handling routine claims for action. Where the targets of a programme are readily identified social groups, such as unemployed youths or elderly people waiting for cataract operations, official statistics will indicate the extent to which the problem a programme addresses is getting better or worse.

The simplest form of evidence-based evaluation of a programme is to compare the latest results with those of the previous year. If there is a consensus about what constitutes good news, evidence that the number of unemployed youths is falling or the waiting time for hospital operations is being cut implies the success of a programme. Attention can also focus on the cost of running a programme. As long as costs are not rising, or rising no faster than benefits, this can be regarded as satisfactory. When quantitative evidence indicates a programme is performing satisfactorily, there is no need for busy policymakers to indulge in foreign comparisons.

Satisficing: it's good enough

Policymakers never have enough time to search for the best programme to address a concern; they are satisfied if programmes are good enough. Herbert Simon (1979: 503) has described this approach to public policy as 'satisficing'. In order to satisfice, a policy does not have to be a world-beater; it is good enough if its performance is consistent with expectations. As long as a programme meets expectations, it can run by routine.

Even if the evidence shows the results of a programme in an unfavourable light – for example, youth unemployment is rising – officials responsible may argue that they are doing the best they can in circumstances in which adult unemployment is rising too. If spending on a programme is cut, officials can justify the resulting cuts in services as a necessary condition of achieving another goal, such as keeping taxes down. Beneficiaries of an established programme tend to share the interests of policymakers in charge. In addition to defending the status quo as good, they can argue that the programme would be better still if it were given a bigger budget in order to produce more of the same, for example, more child care services or a higher pension for retired people. If evidence from other countries is cited indicating that programmes elsewhere are performing better in dealing with a common problem, it can be ignored as long as the established programme is considered good enough as is.

Complacency

The stronger the commitment to the status quo, the greater the likelihood of satisfaction turning into complacency, the unexamined belief that what has produced satisfaction in the past will continue to produce satisfaction. Having a position of power or influence encourages self-satisfaction among officeholders, and the longer a party is in office, the greater the risk of governors suffering from hardening of the political arteries, that is, the complacent belief that whatever they are doing must be the best. Whereas in medieval times religious-inspired *memento mori* (reminders of death) were found in public places to puncture complacency among the powerful, officeholders today are surrounded by go-fers playing to the vanity of their bosses and spin doctors promoting 'good-news' stories designed to smother signs of popular dissatisfaction.

Laws can require an annual report by policymakers on the performance of the programmes for which they are responsible, but the department preparing it will do its best to make it a good-news report. The annual report that Tony Blair issued in the first few years of his New Labour government was consistent with his campaign style: it was a people-centred document full of colour photographs and glossy layouts with lots of white space and little hard evidence. In past decades American legislatures have tried to force the review of programmes through 'sunset' laws that terminate a programme automatically after a fixed period of years if a positive vote is not taken to extend its life. However, such laws have lost favour, as the political pain of terminating an existing programme is very great.

Any attempt to challenge existing programmes by citing foreign successes can be dismissed as irrelevant by officeholders who owe their position to success in national politics. Since Swedish and Norwegian voters do not elect an American president, positive references in Washington to their programmes can be dismissed on the grounds that 'We are not Sweden or Norway.' A leading British politician, R.A. Butler, once dismissed a proposal for parliamentary reform with a patronizing slur on both French and American political practices, calling it an invitation to 'government *à la Americaine*'.

The problem is under control

The level of satisfaction with a programme can drop because of neglect by policymakers or because of unexpected national or international events. When that happens, one way to restore satisfaction is to lower expectations by blaming forces outside the control of government. For example, if the OPEC cartel pushes up the price of oil on world markets, the minister nominally in charge can realistically argue that the government can do nothing to reduce oil prices. However, blaming foreigners is a tacit admission that the government cannot control events, and in big countries proud policymakers do not like to admit that they are outside the decisionmaking loop. Even if the cause of dissatisfaction is outside the control of the national government, its officials expect and are expected to make an effective response.

The first aim of a fire department is to prevent fires occurring; to that end it has programmes of education and inspection designed to reduce this risk. But such measures are never 100 per cent effective. Thus, to complement fire prevention measures, there is a programme for training firemen to fight fires. When a fire breaks out, the object is not to deny the existence of a problem, but to put the fire out with a minimum of damage to property and without loss of life. The immediate aim of the fire chief after arriving at the scene of a blaze is to be able to announce: 'We have things under control.' This is the aim of all public officials when confronted with fires in their in-tray.

If the cause of dissatisfaction appears familiar, policymakers will reach for a familiar remedy. The reasoning is simple: if this remedy worked before, it will work again. As long as familiar methods continue to bring success, the outbreak of a fire is a cause not to introduce new programmes but to apply methods that have delivered satisfaction before. For example, if the waiting list for admission to hospital lengthens, then health officials can argue that their programmes are basically sound, and everything will once again be under control – if budget officials will only give them more money to recruit doctors and nurses from abroad, train more doctors and nurses at home, and build more hospitals so that they have more resources to operate programmes as satisfactorily as before. This assumes that an established programme can continue to produce satisfaction, as long as it is given more resources; this is the view of many defenders of the British National Health Service, established in 1948, and of American programmes established in the 1960s. While budget officials prefer to say no to requests for more money, a government confronted with dissatisfaction with hospitals may decide to throw money at the problem rather than abandon a programme that has produced satisfaction in the past.

Events create problems

Assumptions about what will happen in future are embedded in every public programme. The assumption that nothing will change in a programme or the environment in which it is embedded is convenient, because it eliminates the need to worry about things going wrong. However, the flux of contemporary society implies that all programmes are vulnerable to being disrupted by unexpected events. While risks are usually insufficient to make policymakers start searching for a better programme elsewhere, risks can stimulate awareness that programmes are not bomb-proof in the metaphorical sense – and in the realm of national security, a risk can turn into a deadly reality. While government requires motorists to buy insurance against the risk of an automobile accident, policymakers are much less likely to insure against the risk of their own programmes going wrong. As long as a risk is not realized, a potential problem remains a non-event.

However remote the likelihood, there is always the possibility that something can go wrong with even the most satisfactory of programmes. Assumption-based planning can be used to anticipate risks that can occur and prepare contingency plans for prompt and effective response if the unfortunate happens. It forces policymakers to realize that many of their beliefs are probabilities, not certainties. The object of recognizing risk is to identify preventive measures that can be taken to reduce risks, so that unwanted events do not happen (Box 2.1). For example, building codes specify standards of construction intended to make office blocks fire-proof, and buildings are routinely inspected to enforce fire prevention measures. A second benefit of recognizing risk is that contingency plans can be put in place to protect against their worst effects. 'Fire-proof' buildings are still required to have fire escapes, and these staircases saved the lives of thousands of people working in the World Trade Center on September 11, 2001.

Assumption-based thinking is about contingencies rather than prediction. Instead of claiming that dissatisfaction with a programme will rise, it raises the question: what would happen if things did go wrong? While it does not spread dissatisfaction, it does spread doubt.

Politicians prefer a rosy scenario to the dark clouds of doubt. Warnings of unwelcome events can be dismissed with the statement, 'It hasn't happened yet.' Even if a politician accepts that there are contingent risks in a programme, since an elected official's term of office is relatively limited, he or she can decide to do nothing by calculating, 'It won't happen while I am around.' For example, if a disastrous flood has a probability of occurring once every fifty years, then up to two dozen politicians can be responsible for flood control before a dam finally bursts.

Sooner or later, risks become realities, creating urgent problems for policymakers. The only question is when this happens. Road, railway, and airline

---

Box 2.1 Reducing surprises by questioning assumptions

Although there is always the risk of unexpected events making things go wrong, policymakers prefer to think of things going right. Thus, a plan showing how a programme will operate normally points to its success. The risk of failure has not disappeared; it has only been suppressed.

Assumption-based planning confronts policymakers with the question: what could go wrong? To answer this question, policymakers must look at all the things that *must* happen to bring about success and discriminate between conditions that are virtually certain to be met (for example, the army will remain under civilian control) and conditions based on an assumption that may not be realized (for example, an enemy will not fight a pitched battle but surrender quickly and then fight an underground operation against occupation forces).

Once policymakers recognize that conditions necessary for success cannot be taken for granted, it is possible to protect a programme against risk. For example, a hydroelectric power station generating electricity from the flow of water through a dam is vulnerable to a drought causing its renewable source of energy to dry up. Contingency arrangements can guard against this risk, for example, by enlarging a reservoir to hold water needed if a drought occurs or by building power lines to import electricity from a generating station that does not rely on hydroelectric power. Contingency plans cannot prevent unwanted events from happening but they can go some way towards neutralizing their negative consequences.

Source: Adapted from Dewar, 2002.

---

accidents are unfortunate but familiar examples of events disrupting routine, notwithstanding many accident prevention and safety measures. Bad news creates a crisis in which action is demanded. If blame for the disaster is assigned to individual officeholders, they may be dismissed while their programme remains intact. However, if the programme itself is thought to be at fault, then policymakers must search outside the loop for a new measure.

National governments respond differently to threatening events. After 9/11 the United States government has given the highest priority to introducing new anti-terrorist programmes, while European governments have not. Within Europe there are different responses to risk, too. Sweden's governors have long considered that they are proof against the violence of the United States and treated the assassination of the prime minister on a Stockholm street in 1986 as a unique event. The assassination of the country's foreign minister in 2003 showed that security problems are recurring. Britain's governors have not taken so relaxed an attitude, since in the past quarter-century attacks by the Irish Republican Army almost killed Margaret Thatcher and did kill three Conservative MPs. Tony Blair's high-profile campaign against terrorists

---

Box 2.2 Guarding against the risk of assassination

A president or prime minister, by virtue of the office, is especially vulnerable to assassination, as modern American history demonstrates. In response to the rise of technologically sophisticated international terrorism, British security officials have looked to Washington for lessons about how an assassin could strike and what precautions could be taken. The result has been turning Tony Blair's official Jaguar into a mobile fortress with features such as:

- Armour plating to withstand the blast of a hand grenade or high-velocity automatic rifle bullets.
- Specially designed wheels allowing a fast escape if tyres are punctured by bullets.
- Air cylinder to provide oxygen in case of a gas attack.
- Armour-plating of fuel tank to prevent fire or explosion.
- Special suspension system for carrying at speeds of 150 miles per hour the three tons of weight added by these features.

Source: Adapted from Leppard, 2003.

---

has raised additional security threats. In these circumstances, British security forces have looked to Washington for lessons. The result is a new level of high-technology protection for the prime minister (Box 2.2).

Unexpected events sometimes can have positive consequences for policy. For generations national governments had programmes that raised significant public revenue from the sale of tobacco and programmes that cared for people terminally ill from cancer. When medical research showed the link between smoking and cancer, this was bad news for people who were regular smokers but good news for policymakers, because it pointed to actions that government could take to promote health by reducing the amount that people smoked: boosting the price of cigarettes by raising tobacco taxes, and restricting smoking in public places. Since the results of medical research have travelled quickly around the world, national policymakers have been able to draw lessons from the tobacco control legislation of other countries when preparing their own measures (Studlar, 2004).

Solutions make it easier to face up to problems

When officials in charge of a programme get feedback indicating that things are not going the same as usual, they can learn by puzzling why this is (Heclo, 1974: 304ff.). Because they are close to the action, officials see signs of difficulties well before there is public expression of discontent. They can respond by applying a measure that has worked before. However, if a routine response does not remove signs of difficulty, policymakers face a double puzzle: what is making a programme no longer operate by routine? And what can be done about it?

While puzzlement and dissatisfaction can stimulate action, there is a major weakness: they fail to give guidance about what to do next. Policymakers find it easier to accept evidence of difficulties if it is coupled with a proposed solution. As long as the new proposal is both credible and acceptable to the government of the day, then policymakers have an incentive to listen to critics, because they are not only facing up to a problem but also prepared to tackle it with a fresh solution. In the absence of a solution, politicians have an incentive to continue denying that there is anything wrong or to search for solutions inside the loop.

Together, benchmarking and best-practice analysis offer means of challenging complacency *and* identifying programmes that can improve performance. This is done by comparing the achievements of programmes dealing with a common problem in many countries.

Benchmarking performance

Benchmarking simultaneously offers a means of evaluating a national programme and learning about programmes elsewhere. The intention of benchmarking is constructive: to evaluate a programme's performance by a measure independent of the opinions of policymakers. In the absence of such an external stimulus, policymakers can regard an existing programme as satisfactory without any evidence to support their judgement. Evaluating a programme against a benchmark standard will show whether, or to what extent, satisfaction is justified. Insofar as the results are positive, the process endorses the predisposition to ignore what is done abroad. But insofar as benchmarking shows that a programme producing domestic satisfaction is not so successful as others evaluated by the same standard, benchmarking can stimulate policymakers to adopt improvements by learning from comparable countries that do do better (Lundvall and Tomlinson, 2002; Rose, 2003a).

The focus of benchmarking is not on the mechanics of a programme but on outcomes. The underlying assumption is that, if a country's performance is rated highly in the benchmarking process, a programme associated with it is satisfactory. Benchmarking rejects the social scientist's practice of explaining differences in performance as due to differences in national context and resources. Instead, it emphasizes that substandard performance implies a need to improve a national programme; this makes it a spur to low-achieving governments to do better.

The first step in benchmarking is to agree a standard for comparing programme outcomes. The measure is usually quantified, for example, the number of infants per thousand who die in childbirth; the number of adolescents meeting a given examination standard in numeracy; or the percentage of airline flights completing a journey within ten minutes of their published arrival time. As these examples show, benchmarking can be applied in many different programme contexts.

Programmes can be benchmarked by a pass/fail standard which any number can pass, provided that they meet the specified standard. For example, the European Central Bank, which is responsible for the euro, benchmarks the performance of each national government in supporting price stability, using criteria such as the size of the government's budget deficit (Issing *et al.*, 2001). In principle, all national governments could and should meet its benchmark standard of keeping the deficit below 3 per cent of the country's gross domestic product. The benchmark standard is not only a target for national governors to aim at but also a means of identifying national governments that fail to meet the anti-inflation benchmark.

A simple pass/fail standard does not distinguish between degrees of success, since some programmes will perform well above the pass rate, while others will just scrape by. A simple way to provide more information is to group the performance of national programmes into three categories: average, above average, and below average. This tripartite classification avoids the all-or-nothing judgement that a programme is either good or failing. Instead, it recognizes that the performance of many countries can be 'middling'. For example, Freedom House benchmarks the performance of each UN member government according to standards of civil and political liberties, and then assigns each country to one of three categories: free, partly free, or unfree. The tripartite evaluation of performance gives many policymakers a degree of satisfaction from the fact that their programmes are average, while there is a prod to do better because their performance is not as good as countries in the above-average group.

Since benchmarking is about encouraging policymakers to do better, it makes sense to create categories that are like rungs in a ladder of progress. This technique is particularly well suited for making global comparisons. There is little point in showing that the performance of African countries in health or education lags behind Europe: the critical task for African policymakers is to move up to the next rung on the ladder. The approach is being used in international evaluations of e-government, since national governments have introduced the Internet to public administration at different times, and most are still expanding its coverage (Box 2.3).

When a United Nations team benchmarked the extent of e-government in 2001, it was taking a snapshot when a motion picture was more desirable. Therefore, it was not sensible to describe countries in terms of static categories such as being on one or the other side of a digital divide, since any standard fixed could be surpassed by dozens of countries by the time of the evaluation. Instead, the benchmark categories emphasized the movement from inaction to the emergence of programmes; then to the enhancement of programmes; and, once e-government capability is widespread, upgrading Internet services to

---

Box 2.3 Benchmarking stages of development: e-government around the world

Extent to which e-government services are available, 2001

No action taken.   21 countries.

Emerging.   An official government online presence is established: 32 countries.

Enhanced.   Government sites increase; information becomes more dynamic: 65 countries.

Interactive.   Users can download forms from the web and exchange e-mails with officials: 57 countries.

Transactional.   Users can actually pay for services and request and receive licenses and permits online: 17 countries.

Seamless.   Full integration of e-services across government agencies: 0 countries.

Source: United Nations, Department of Public Economics and Public Administration, 2003, 2.

---

interactive web sites and web sites through which transactions can be made on line. The UN ladder did not treat the best-performing e-government countries as already at the top; it had one rung that none had yet reached, the seamless integration of Internet links across administrative boundaries dividing government agencies from each other.

Benchmarking can also be used to create a league table in which the performance of all countries is ranked by a single indicator from the highest to the lowest. Whereas a pass/fail or categoric standard reduces differences between individual countries by grouping them in one or another category, a league table tends to exaggerate differences between countries, for each step in the ranking from the top of the league is perceived as a big step down. For example, if the achievements of twenty-five European Union member states are compared, the country ranked eighth will appear far from the top, even though it is in the upper third, and a country ranked fifteenth will appear unsuccessful, even though its performance is benchmarked in the middle third of countries.

In a league-table ranking, as in a sporting competition, the size of the gap between countries is unimportant. The programme associated with the most successful outcome is identified in the media as the 'winner' of a European Cup or Olympic competition for the best programme in a given field. However, the same policy does not apply in public policy. The difference between the EU country ranked first and twelfth in a league table of infant mortality, for example, is 0.25 per cent, that is, the difference between 996.5 live births and 994.0 live births per thousand.

Best practice – for better or for worse?

Whereas benchmarking compares how different governments are doing, the intent of best-practice analysis is to show what governments ought to do. The best-practice approach is positive in the highest degree: it identifies a single programme as the best and challenges other governments to move outside the loop and import it. The best programme is usually assumed to be that in effect in the country at the top of a league table. This is not the only possible explanation of why a country leads the league. Its top performance, say, in health may be due to a superior programme or it may largely be due to other circumstances, such as the healthy behaviour of its population. Since the promoters of best practice are usually action-oriented management consultants rather than cautious social scientists, such qualifications are usually ignored.

While comparisons across countries offer a 'thick' bundle of information, the evidence used to determine which programme is best is 'thin': a single quantitative indicator determines the ranking in a league table. While a quantitative ranking appears precise, it is also inadequate when the different outcomes associated with a programme's performance cannot be reduced to a single number. For example, a good cost/benefit ratio says nothing about how a programme achieves a high standard of efficiency: it may be by spending a lot of money very effectively or it can be by financing cheap programmes with limited low-cost effects. Detailed knowledge is usually absent in the interpretation of international league tables.

If there is a political consensus, qualitative judgements can be substituted for quantitative rankings in determining best practice. At an international meeting, national ministers can observe that country X is successful in terms of achieving A. From this, the inference is drawn that success is due to the superiority of its particular programme, and that becomes the consensus example of international best practice. For example, for four decades economic policymakers attributed Germany's success in achieving high economic growth and low inflation to the institutional independence and policies of the German Bundesbank. Other possible causes, such as technical skills of workers, long-term outlooks of investment bankers, and a low level of public spending on military defence, were ignored. So strong was the perceived association between the German central bank and economic success that it became the best-practice model for the twelve-country European Central Bank.

The identification of a single programme as superior to all others is unnecessarily restrictive. It creates a positional good, since at any one time only a single country's programme can hold the top position (Hirsch, 1977). Media headlines can even label national policies as having 'failed' to achieve the best when the difference between being top and second, third, or fourth can be slight in absolute terms. Best-practice prescriptions tend to homogenize distinctions between programmes ranging from the second-best to the worst. Yet in countries where programmes are currently below average, the logic of transitive progress is that average practice is an improvement on substandard performance and that 'second-best practice' would be better still. However, from the perspective of policy entrepreneurs, promoting second-best practice is a harder sell than promoting best practice. Doing so invites opposition not only from those against any change but also from idealists asking: why not the best?

Concentrating attention exclusively on best practice overlooks the benefits of learning from worst practice. A better understanding of the causes of failure in other countries can help governors avoid politically fatal mistakes – and learning vicariously about failure is far less costly than learning from failure in practice. Whereas Mikhail Gorbachev essayed an experiment in economic and political transformation 'unlike that of any other country in history', the leaders of the People's Republic of China are opening up their economy with full knowledge of the measures that led to the collapse of the Soviet Union under Gorbachev. The benefits to China's rulers of learning from the Soviet failure are as great or greater than the advantages the Chinese might gain from following best-practice prescriptions from the world's richest economies.

One problem with many solutions

Best practice and benchmarking have a common starting point: the comparative evaluation of programmes addressing a common objective. Because of this, the two are often confused. For example, the best-practice website of the British Cabinet Office does not define best practice: it directs searchers to another site, www.benchmarking.gov.uk, which states that its purpose is 'improving ourselves by learning from others'. However, the two methods do have important differences in the way they evaluate programmes and draw lessons for improvement.

Because best-practice analysis spotlights a league leader, it throws in the shadows alternative ways of improving performance. By contrast, benchmarking gives equal attention to the programmes of all governments in the top category; it thus offers a plurality of examples of how a higher standard of performance can be achieved. Whereas best-practice analysis points to a 'one-size-fits-all' diagnosis and prescription, benchmarking offers national policymakers a menu of programmes to choose from. For example, Harvard Professor Robert Putnam's website established to promote the use of social capital to improve local programmes, www.bettertogether.org, does not rank local performance, as a best-practice analysis would; it simply offers lots of examples of programmes associated with positive outcomes. Likewise, the annual *World Development Report* of the World Bank (e.g. 2002a) categorizes countries in four broad categories –

low-income, lower-middle-income, upper-middle-income, and high-income countries – rather than ranking countries in a global league table from 1st to 181st. In addition, each *Report* has a profusion of boxes that give succinct prose descriptions of programmes employed by developing countries benchmarked as successful.

Since any policy outcome may be influenced by several programmes and many programmes have multiple objectives, there are good reasons to profile a country's performance with separate evaluations for different goals. Benchmarking according to multiple indicators is particularly important in global comparisons. For example, countries that are relatively poor in absolute terms of cash income may, for just this reason, achieve faster rates of economic growth. If absolute levels of GDP per capita are used to rank national economies, the People's Republic of China appears poor. However, if attention is shifted to the annual rate of economic growth, then China is a world leader (World Bank, 2002c).

The use of multiple criteria is also appropriate when countries giving foreign aid want to combine grants of money with conditions for receiving and spending. From a best-practice perspective, the conditions for receiving a grant should be narrowly specified, focusing attention on a single programme. The International Monetary Fund tends to favour this approach, recommending programmes effective in reducing inflation, whatever the secondary effects of doing so. By contrast, a benchmarking approach offers a country seeking advice and money a menu of alternative programmes associated with different ways of achieving a goal, and with different secondary costs and benefits. Similarly, the ladder-of-progress approach to e-government usually shows that the type of programme requuired to advance the next stage up a ladder depends on where a country is at present.

Paradoxically, the lower a country is in a benchmarked comparison, the wider the choice of countries it can turn to in search of learning lessons that can be used to improve its own performance. While the non-directive approach of benchmarking offers a wide choice of possible solutions, it also faces busy policymakers with a new problem: where to look?

Step 3
Where to look for lessons

Humani nil a me alienum puto.
(Nothing that concerns man is alien to me.)
Terence, *c.* 160 BC

The only condition limiting where to look for lessons is the existence of a common problem. When national policymakers are confronted by a problem that is new to them, this does not mean it is unprecedented; it may simply indicate they are the last to become aware of what is already familiar elsewhere. For example, race relations was not regarded as a problem in Britain until the 1960s, because the country was previously almost 100 per cent white. The arrival of immigrants from the West Indies and the Indian subcontinent changed that. Before responding with legislation, British policymakers looked to the United States for examples of programmes, since race relations is an old problem there.

A limited number of problems are abnormal in the statistical sense of not confronting most governments. Bilingualism, for example, is a major concern in only six of thirty OECD countries – Belgium, Canada, Finland, Ireland, Luxembourg, and Switzerland. Other programmes are context-dependent: for example, programmes to develop rural areas do not concern cities. But only a 'country' as small as the Vatican City is without any rural area. Since urban and rural differences divide every country, rural American states such as North Dakota and Montana may look to neighbouring Canadian provinces for ideas about rural development rather than to Washington, Chicago, or New York.

When you are dissatisfied with a programme, a solution can be sought by canvassing for ideas within the national policy network. This can be followed up by the construction of a novel programme based on assumptions about how it could work. Yet, however careful this speculative exercise is, no one can say whether it could work in practice because it is 'too novel', that is, it has never been put into effect. By contrast, if you turn your attention to what other countries are doing about a common problem, it is possible to see how different programmes actually do work.

   Although circumstances can push you to search elsewhere for lessons, they do not determine where you look. Every national government is today embedded in a host of formal and informal links with other countries. For example, Britain is a member of the European Union, but policymakers have a psychologically important special relationship with the United States and, depending on the political colour of British government, there may be an ideological affinity with social democrats in Sweden or free market groups in the United States.

   'Go where you are comfortable' is an easy rule to follow. It also explains why national governments may not turn to neighbours if they are very different in resources and political history. While Japan has no hesitancy in learning lessons from the West, it has never looked to its nearest geographical neighbour, Russia, for inspiration. Nor do Koreans with a memory of generations of Japanese occupation look there for ideas. Likewise, Australians feel more comfortable looking to Britain or the United States than to their neighbours in Indonesia and Papua New Guinea. 'Go where you can learn something useful' is a rule that underscores the instrumental character of lesson-drawing; it can lead to visits to distant and unfamiliar places.

   The transnational flow of information through formal and informal political channels means there is no shortage of places where policymakers might look. However, busy people do not have enough time to examine more than one or two examples of what has been done elsewhere. The simplest thing to do is to search past history for analogies with a new problem. But as the next section of this chapter shows, your conclusions depend on which bits of which past are selected for your analogy. When attention is turned to foreign countries, the choices are between friendly and familiar countries and useful strangers. Familiar countries may offer limited stimulus because their programmes are similar to your own. By contrast, the programmes of countries that are unfamiliar are more likely to offer fresh and challenging insights precisely because they are distant and different. The concluding section examines the attractive power of countries that develop smart programmes; it also looks at circumstances in which powerful countries can impose dumb programmes on others. Given the plenitude of places to look for lessons, there is no one best country as a source of ideas for programmes. Where you look should follow from what you want to learn.

Uses and limits of history

A knowledge of history can help policymakers understand the programmes they currently administer, for an established programme is not their choice but the legacy of choices made and modified through many decades. Understanding who did what, when, and why is useful knowledge if one is confronted with changing a programme. As the economic historian Joseph Schumpeter (1946: 1) has noted:

In order to understand the religious events from 1520 to 1530 or the political events from 1780 to 1800 or the developments in painting from 1900
to 1910, you must survey a period of much wider span. Not to do so is the
hallmark of dilettantism.

When Tony Blair became prime minister of Britain in 1997, he proclaimed
the ambition to make everything 'new, new, new', as if commitments to the
National Health Service since 1948 or underinvestment in public transport
under Margaret Thatcher in the 1980s could be ignored. After years in office,
Blair has learned the power of the past.

Historical analogies as quasi-lessons

When policymakers speak of the 'lessons' of history, they are not referring to
what they learned as students; instead, they are relying on selected examples
from the past to justify current action. An analogy offers a simple and fast
method for drawing a lesson from the past. Historical analogies fasten on a
prominent characteristic that both the past and the current problem have in
common – and assume that both share other characteristics as well. If the earlier
problem was resolved successfully, the analogy provides positive knowledge to
guide current decisions about future actions. If the outcome was disastrous, an
analogy indicates what not to do. Lesson-drawing by analogy does not require
historical research; detailed historical knowledge may even be an obstacle to
drawing the lesson that is sought from the past.

Analogies are frequently invoked in foreign policy by officials facing unexpected problems in unfamiliar parts of the world. In an attempt to comprehend
an unfamiliar situation and an incomprehensible adversary, policymakers
can relate the novel challenge facing them to one or more situations with which
they are already familiar (Khong, 1992; Hemmer, 2000). Analogical reasoning
appeals since policymakers in foreign affairs are likely to be educated in history
or law, both disciplines that encourage looking to the past for precedents, rather
than in rational choice economics, which analyses problems by deducing causes
from abstract principles devoid of historical context.

The process of drawing an analogy starts with the identification of a past
situation that has one or more similarities with the present (Box 3.1). Since
history is a vast warehouse of events, there is no shortage of materials from the
past. For a situation to be adopted as an analogy, there must be sufficient similarities between past and present events so that the present difficulty can be
framed and interpreted in the light of past experience. While this reduces the
number of analogies relevant to a given current problem, it is usually possible
to find a multiplicity of contrasting events that have one or more features that
are analogous to the present. For example, after the Egyptian government
nationalized the Suez Canal in 1956, the British prime minister, Sir Anthony

---

Box 3.1 Simple steps in making a historical analogy

First: Identify similarities between a past situation and a current problem: for example, the buildup of arms by Nazi Germany and the build up of nuclear power by North Korea.

Second: Frame and describe the current problem in terms of the past situation: just as Nazi Germany wanted to regain a former German territory, so North Korea is seen as seeking control of the whole of Korea.

Third: Make a forecast by analogy with the past: rearmament is an aggressive act leading to war.

Fourth: Draw a conclusion about how to act: non-resistance to military buildups will lead to world war (the Munich analogy), while prompt resistance will prevent the spread of war (the 1950–1953 Korean War analogy).

Fifth: Use the analogy rhetorically: aggression must be stopped; we don't want another Munich in Asia.

Sixth: Ignore similarities with other past events that imply contrary actions: the growth of Chinese and Japanese military and economic power may be frightening North Korea, or a dictator may appear aggressive internationally to boost domestic support.

Eden, drew an analogy with Hitler's seizure of lands in Central Europe. By contrast, the Egyptian leader, Gamal Abdel Nasser, drew an analogy with the action of newly independent governments in other third-world countries to nationalize properties owned by their former rulers. Debates about the appropriate analogy for framing events often occur within government. For example, debates in Washington about sending American troops into action often lead to conflicting analogies between 'hawks', who cite successes in places such as Grenada and Kuwait, and 'doves', who make analogies with failure in Vietnam.

Once an analogy is established between a past and present difficulty, the past is used to preview how the current problem is likely to develop. When policymakers invoke an analogy with 'Munich', they are not so much thinking about negotiations there in 1938 but of the consequences of the Munich agreement. It sought to appease Hitler's territorial demands but, instead of bringing 'peace in our time' as Prime Minister Neville Chamberlain promised, it was followed within a year by the outbreak of the Second World War. Likewise, when American policymakers describe a current difficulty as another Vietnam, the implication is that the commitment of American troops will last for years and cost tens of thousands of American lives. The forecast provided by an analogy prescribes what to do or what not to do. President Harry Truman justified his 1950 decision to commit American troops to the defence of the Republic of Korea when it was invaded by North Korea:

> I recalled some earlier instances: Manchuria, Ethiopia, Austria. I remembered how each time that the democracies failed to act it had encouraged the aggressors to keep going ahead. Communism was acting in Korea just as Hitler, Mussolini and the Japanese had acted ten, fifteen and twenty years earlier. I felt certain that if South Korea was allowed to fall, Communist leaders would be emboldened to override nations closer to our own shores. If the Communists were permitted to force their way into the Republic of Korea without opposition from the free world, no small nation would have the courage to resist threats and aggression by stronger Communist neighbors. If this was allowed to go unchallenged, it would mean a Third World War, just as similar incidents had brought on the Second World War.
>
> (Truman, 1956: 332–333)

More than 2,500 years ago the Greek historian Heraclitus wrote, 'You can't step into the same river twice.' In the literal sense, the statement is true, but in the practical sense it is a half-truth, for statutory commitments in such fields as pensions result in many programmes continuing through the force of political inertia. Yet sooner or later every programme is likely to reach a point at which social, economic, and political changes make discontinuities with the past more important than continuities. At that point, analogies with the past become dangerous.

A danger in drawing lessons from history is that it will lead to conclusions valid about the past but no longer valid today. This is the ghost that haunts military strategists, for a great deal of military training is devoted to the analysis of past military battles. Losers have particular incentives to learn from their defeats, and victors have good reason to be sure they understand the causes of their successes. However, advances in technology and military tactics mean that fighting the previous war is no guarantee that the next war will be fought in the same way. The Maginot Line in France is a textbook example of applying past lessons to current risks. After the First World War, France built the heavily fortified Maginot Line along its border with Germany. When Germany attacked France, the Maginot Line held firm, but France fell because the German army outflanked it by invading through Belgium (Box 3.2).

The everyday activity of policymakers is not understanding the past but understanding the present. Abstracting a few points from the past can lead to heroic or foolhardy assumptions about the predictive value of past events. A course of action justified by an analogy can be challenged by invoking an

---

Box 3.2 The risk of re-fighting past wars

The German invasion of France in the First World War resulted in parts of France becoming a battlefield for four years and the loss of hundreds of thousands of French lives. After France emerged on the winning side, the French government vowed that never again would so many French die as a result of a German invasion. In the 1920s and 1930s France invested great sums of money and materials in constructing the Maginot Line along the Franco-German border. The line consisted of a complex of closely linked trenches and fortifications with heavy artillery sufficient to repulse a German attack by infantry, tanks, or the airpower of that era.

When the Second World War broke out in September 1939, the Maginot Line held firm against German forces. However, in May 1940, Belgium and Luxembourg fell to a *Blitzkrieg* attack by the German army. Since the Maginot Line did not extend to France's borders with Belgium, German troops were able to advance rapidly across northern France. While the Maginot Line remained firm on France's eastern border, the German invasion through Belgium led to the surrender of France and German troops entering Paris a month later.

Source: See Rowe, 1959.

---

alternative analogy prescribing a different course. When there are signs of rising inflation and of rising unemployment, political economists often invoke analogies with German history to justify their policy priority. Monetarists argue that it is necessary to give priority to fighting inflation because the German hyperinflation of the early 1920s was followed by Hitler taking power in 1933. By contrast, Keynesians give priority to fighting unemployment, because Hitler's seizure of power followed a big rise in German unemployment during the world depression. The first analogy overlooks the fact that German inflation was followed by a period of prosperity under Gustav Stresemann, who was awarded the Nobel prize for peace in 1926. The Keynesian analogy overlooks the fact that during the depression unemployment also rose in countries that did not turn to fascism, such as Britain and the United States.

When there is a disagreement within government about what to do, alternative analogies will be scrutinized for their implications for action rather than for historical completeness or accuracy. At that point the choice between analogies is not a search for historical similarities but for examples that will point in the 'right' direction, that is, the direction favoured by policymakers. Once a government decides whether to invoke the threat of force rather than stand aside from entanglement in a foreign battlefield, it can then choose to invoke the 'Munich' or the 'Vietnam' analogy as a rhetorical device to mobilize support for its chosen course. Analogies can also be used to discredit those who disagree, for instance, suggesting that opponents of the use of force are equivalent to appeasers of Hitler, or that those who want to use force would send troops into a quagmire as deadly as Vietnam.

The 'lessons' produced from historical analogies are *quasi*-lessons, because they are not systematically thought through but depend on a few selected similarities. To draw a proper lesson would require a detailed and systematic examination of the past in order to understand what happened and why. The interpretation of the past is the professional job of historians. While a few historians become media celebrities by prescribing policies based on analogies with the past, when doing so they are not acting as historians but as media pundits. Many professional historians are shy about using historical analogies to support current policies and even hesitant about drawing conclusions about centuries-old events. For example, even though the French Revolution began in 1789 and the English Revolution more than a century earlier, there are continuing debates among historians about how to interpret their causes and consequences.

Learning from afar as well as near at hand

Serendipity – accidentally hearing about an interesting programme abroad – is one way in which policymakers decide where to look for a lesson. But the unplanned nature of the process poses the question: how do you build serendipity into lesson-drawing? Although the learning of policymakers is often accidental, it is not random. Policymakers are embedded in a multiplicity of networks based on proximity and power. In today's world, telecommunications and jet aeroplanes shrink distance; the result is that proximity is defined not only or not so much by geography as it is by historical ties and similarities in political culture. Officials wanting to learn about programmes elsewhere can look across continents as well as near at hand.

Neighbours and distant friends

In policymaking as in friendship, there is a tendency to communicate most with friends and neighbours who share many experiences in common. Local mayors have no difficulty in relating to mayors of other cities like their own. In a federal system, the governors of states or the minister-presidents of German *Länder* share a common interest in programmes that will improve their region and prevent the federal government from strengthening its powers against themselves. While presidents and prime ministers head different countries, they share similar problems of keeping on top of their national government. They also appreciate the fact that foreign leaders, unlike their domestic colleagues, are not out to get their job.

Scandinavian countries are a prime example of having national governments that are both friends and neighbours. Because of a legacy of common rule by the same crown, they have much in common historically and institutionally. Because they are all small, they share concerns about their more populous neighbours. Moreover, all are prosperous and have large welfare state programmes funded by high levels of taxation. The Nordic Council was founded in 1952 to institutionalize the exchange of information about programmes between policymakers in Denmark, Finland, Iceland, Norway, and Sweden.

Contacts among English-speaking countries are an outstanding example of historical links and contemporary interests triumphing over geographical distance. In the days of sailing ships, the British Empire established a network extending across continents to Canada, Australia, and New Zealand. Since the United States and Britain became allies in the Second World War, Washington too has become a member of an English-speaking network of governments communicating through e-mail, by telephone, and by jet as readily as Nordic countries were communicating across much shorter distances by train and ferry. The exclusion from the network of Ireland and of West Indian countries, not to mention Scandinavian countries where policymakers may be as fluent in English as their counterparts in Ottawa, is a reminder that shared political values can create policy networks across continents.

Useful strangers

Relying on people just like us is often an obstacle to learning new lessons (Rogers, 1995: 18ff., 286ff.). The fewer the differences between programmes of two governments, the fewer new ideas or techniques are available. It leads to non-learning, insofar as the only information that people just like us can offer is no different from what you know already. While learning from friends can be useful for making adjustments in established programmes, it is an obstacle to breaking outside the loop and learning something new. Introverted policymakers who ignore programmes that are developed by people who are 'not like us' are likely to be ignorant of innovations in many parts of the world.

By contrast, most different countries offer the maximum of fresh insights into public policy. Late nineteenth-century Japan is a textbook example of the benefits of doing so. After ironclad American ships armed with cannons sailed into a defenceless Meiji harbour in 1854, its officials sought lessons from the rest of the world. Notwithstanding an island culture steeped in tradition, officials travelled to Europe and the United States in search of lessons that would enable Japan to catch up with more industrialized rivals and thereby maintain national independence by 'inventing' a new Japan (Westney, 1987).

Learning from strangers is most useful when similarity in conditions is combined with striking differences in outcome. This was the method that Martin Luther King used to develop his strategy of non-violent resistance to segregation in Montgomery, Alabama. There was no point in King turning to black friends and neighbours in Georgia in the early 1950s, for whites monopolized power

Box 3.3 Long-distance learning: the quest of Martin Luther King

When Martin Luther King was a young undergraduate student at Morehouse College in Atlanta, he read voraciously in search of the meaning of life, as a person who was prepared to dedicate his life to the Christian ministry, and as a black who experienced racial injustice in the segregated Deep South. One of the class reading assignments that particularly impressed him was an essay, 'Civil Disobedience' by Henry David Thoreau, written in 1849 after Thoreau was jailed in Massachusetts for refusing to pay a poll tax on the grounds that he was a conscientious objector to the Mexican–American war, which he saw as an effort to extend slavery.

A few years later at Crozer Theological Seminary in Pennsylvania, King learned about Mahatma Gandhi's doctrine of nonviolent resistance, which Gandhi had used to organize the undermining of Britain's rule in its Indian empire. Gandhi interpreted this doctrine as meaning the refusal to co-operate with evil. Gandhi had adopted this idea after being deeply impressed by reading Thoreau's essay 'Civil Disobedience', and it influenced his strategy of organizing mass protests and the rejection of laws laid down by the ruling British authorities. After more than two decades, Gandhi achieved his goal of India's independence from Britain.

In 1955, shortly after Dr King had become a pastor in Montgomery, Alabama, a black woman, Rosa Parks, was charged with violating a local law because she refused to give up her seat on a bus to a white person. Taking his lead from Gandhi, who in turn had taken a lead from Thoreau, King became leader of the boycott of the Jim Crow bus system in Montgomery. The bus boycott stimulated a civil rights movement that led to changes in American society that hitherto King could only have dreamt about. As in the case of Gandhi, King finally fell victim to an assassin.

Source: On Martin Luther King's early studies, see Oates, 1982, pp. 31ff.

there too. Instead, King looked across oceans to study the passive resistance strategy and tactics developed by the Hindu leader Mohandas K. Gandhi to advance India's demand for independence from the British Empire (Box 3.3).

Notwithstanding striking examples of learning across continents, political culture – that is, the distinctive values, beliefs and emotions, of a country – is often cited as a major or even an insuperable obstacle to drawing lessons across cultures. The argument is flawed insofar as it assumes that any cultural difference will act as a pervasive obstacle to the transfer of all programmes. It is also flawed in failing to recognize that government programmes operate at a different level than underlying cultural values. Cultural values such as pride in country are meant to be widespread and consensual. By contrast, policymakers searching for a programme that works will look at competing alternatives and there will be political disagreement about which to adopt (see Step 7). Politics starts where cultural consensus ends.

   The limits of cultural theories can be seen by looking for something to eat in a busy American shopping centre. Anthropologists make much of the cultural roots of differences in eating habits. But differences in foods can become an attraction. Immigrant groups migrating to the United States from all over the world now offer Americans the opportunity to eat foods from other continents. Pizzas, bagels, and tacos can now claim to be as American as apple pie. The melting-pot nature of American society is reflected in its gastronomic diversity. In addition, McDonald's is a classic example of a very American company succeeding across a hundred different cultures by assuming that, notwithstanding cultural differences, it is possible to make money by applying in foreign countries a business model that has worked at home (Box 3.4). Similarly, countries

---

Box 3.4 If culture is important, why does McDonald's sell hamburgers in 117 countries?

Differences in diet, tastes in food, and meal customs are often ascribed to cultural differences. It is commonplace to speak of French cuisine or American Southern cooking as an expression of a culture. In Italy a 'slow food' movement has been launched to preserve traditional Italian eating habits against the advance of fast food outlets.

   The founders of McDonald's, the American hamburger chain, were not cultural anthropologists but business people. After establishing a successful formula for selling fast food in the United States, they began opening up branches abroad. This meant selling American hamburgers in Hamburg, Germany, from which the name of their chief commodity came, and in places as far afield as Hong Kong and Japan. Today, there are more than 31,000 McDonald's restaurants in 117 countries on six continents. On a typical day, McDonald's serves more than 46 million customers. Nine countries with diverse cultures provide most of its customers: Australia, Brazil, Canada, China, France, Germany, Japan, the United Kingdom, and the United States.

   While Americans sleep, people on other continents are eating at McDonald's. The busiest McDonald's restaurant is not in Chicago but in Moscow, and Russia now ranks second only to the United States in the average number of customers served at a McDonald's restaurant. While the French government seeks to defend its culinary traditions by opening an institute to teach gastronomy and taste to 100 students a year, its citizens regularly eat at the 970 McDonald's restaurants in France. While a meal at McDonald's can have a different social significance in Beijing or Cape Town than in Baltimore or Chicago, this meaning is irrelevant to its shareholders who profit from the worldwide success of this American-based chain.

   Source: McDonald's Corporation, 2003a and 2003b; James L. Watson, 1997.

with a Confucian and Communist cultural mix such as the People's Republic of China or with the strictly Islamic culture of Saudi Arabia do not prevent governments there from learning from other cultures how to create a jet air force and missile system that can strike effectively against potential aggressors from other cultures.

The logic of lesson-drawing is about 'part–part' learning, that is, gaining knowledge about how one specific programme operates in one part of another society, and considering whether it could operate in a similar part of another society. In the words of a comparative lawyer, 'What the law reformer should be after in looking at foreign systems is an idea which could be transformed into part of the law of his country' (quoted in Alan Watson, 1976: 98). In the process of doing so, details that are important to cultural anthropologists, such as its symbolic associations, are removed because they are not directly integral to its effectiveness. Lessons are drawn by learning what to leave out as well as what to include (see Step 5).

Too big or too good to ignore

Countries with best-practice programmes attract attention on the grounds of success while the programmes of powerful countries attract interest because they are too big to ignore. The number of really big countries is few and some, such as Pakistan and Indonesia, have more reasons to learn from abroad than to offer lessons. Moreover, the power of a large army or a rich national treasury or both is not a sufficient motive for policymakers looking to a country for lessons. Small countries, most notably those of Scandinavia, are often cited as examples of best practice in Europe, but their international reach is much less than that of Britain, a relatively large and English-speaking country.

Attractive powers

At the height of the power of the Soviet Union, its military and political power was too great to be ignored by countries forcibly incorporated into the Communist bloc. Communist regimes were locked into a set of economic, social, and military programmes that followed blueprints laid down in Moscow. The peoples of the Baltic states, then an integral part of the Soviet Union, were not allowed to study the causes of the high standards of living in Scandinavia. Nor were East Germans allowed to adopt programmes producing high living standards in West Germany. To show an interest in learning about programmes in advanced industrial societies was evidence of a bourgeois or even anti-state mentality, and risked punishment. Today, Central and East European countries are free to look for lessons where they wish. They usually turn their backs on their Russian neighbour and look to governments in the European Union or across the Atlantic.

Although Sweden is a small, neutral country in international politics, its high living standards and generous social benefits have made it attractive as a source of lessons, especially to social democrats who endorse the Swedish readiness to finance costly programmes through taxes that tend to redistribute income. Equally, proponents of the market are attracted to learn about Sweden in order to use it as a warning of what not to do, because of the high taxes that the Swedish government has had to levy to finance its programmes. Under Margaret Thatcher, Britain attracted international interest because of its pioneering and wide-ranging series of privatization programmes.

Today, the United States combines the attractiveness of both hard and soft power. Hard power is most evident in its military capabilities, which combine high-technology weaponry and more than a million men and women in uniform. The economic power of the United States is evident in the total size of its gross domestic product, in the dollar's role in international financial markets, and in the extent to which American firms attract foreign investments and foreign central banks are ready to loan money to finance the deficit of the federal government. Moreover, the American government can use its leading role in institutions such as the International Monetary Fund and the World Bank to advocate the application of its economic principles and programmes in other countries. The United States' dominant position in NATO can be used to advance military equipment, tactics, and strategies consistent with American practices. In explaining Canadian policies to a Washington audience, its then prime minister, Pierre Trudeau, said:

> Let me say that it should not be surprising if these policies in many instances either reflect or take into account the proximity of the United States. Living next to you is like sleeping with an elephant.
>
> (Quoted in Hoberg, 1991: 108)

Soft power refers to a country having an 'attractive culture' that encourages other countries to want what it wants; 'it co-opts people rather than coercing them' (Nye, 2002: 9). The English language is an example of soft power, for it has attracted use by policymakers. While national parliaments continue to debate in their national language, the head of government and of its central bank and its diplomats usually rely on English when travelling abroad. Publications such as the *Wall Street Journal*, *The Economist*, and the *Financial Times* circulate on every continent. While cosmopolitan in news coverage, such publications give a disproportionate amount of attention to what happens in their country of origin. British diplomats sometimes argue that the worldwide use of English enables Britain, with less economic and military power than the United States, to 'punch above its weight'. The use of English is not, however, a sign of agreement. Its use by Middle East governments does not make them followers of Washington's political lines, and in European Union institutions policymakers can negotiate in English to agree a programme that leaves the British government isolated.

The extent to which the United States today combines both hard and soft power raises the question: is it too big to learn? Internationally powerful countries are more accustomed to lecturing other countries than to listening: national power can be used to 'afford not to learn' (Deutsch, 1963: 111). The more powerful the country, the easier it is politically to dismiss comparisons with smaller countries, even though there is no necessary connection between the size of a country's army and the quality of its health or education services. For example, Soviet leaders cited the country's ability to make nuclear weapons and send rockets to the moon to counter criticisms of its failure to deliver domestic social programmes to the standards of Western Europe. American pre-eminence as a global political and economic power has encouraged the belief that while the United States can import people it need not learn how foreigners think, a belief shaken by terrorist attacks of 9/11 and their aftermath.

No one best country

Lesson-drawing is about programmes rather than about national power; therefore, any attempt to establish a single country, whether the United States or Sweden, as the place to which policymakers should turn for lessons about all forms of public policy is misguided. For example, even though the United States is a leading country for technology, power blackouts in the United States when the demand for electricity surged in summer 2003 led a former American energy secretary to say, 'We're the world's greatest superpower but we have a third-world electricity grid.' Acting on that logic, a delegation from the Federal Energy Regulatory Commission went to India to learn lessons from its successful programme of dealing with power blackouts, which are a recurring problem in its low-technology electricity system (Luce, 2003).

To assume that policymakers look to a single country to learn about how to make their programmes better implies that they have tunnel vision directed at a single country as a source of lessons. In fact, the network of policymakers is more like a cubist painting, for every policymaker is at the intersection of a multiplicity of networks that operate in different dimensions. While this generates multiple political pressures, it also offers multiple sources of information about programmes of other governments in the same policy area. Instead of looking to a single source for information, whether in Washington, Brussels, or Paris, policymakers can learn from the 'polydiffusion' of ideas through the multiple networks in which they are embedded (Mossberger and Hale, 2002).

The logic of benchmarking is that performance counts far more than friendship does. The results of programmes from different countries are set out without regard to geography, culture, or language. The performance of countries from different continents, such as the United States, Japan, and Sweden, may be grouped together, and neighbours such as Germany and Poland may be placed far apart.

Peer group review brings together policymakers whose programmes have been benchmarked by the same standard so that they can learn from each other. While some group members are likely to be friends, others are likely to be strangers. What they have in common is that they are peers, that is, similar in their professional and technical understanding of a specific area of public policy. The benchmarking process divides national programmes into those associated with more and less successful programmes. Learning can take place through an informal exchange of information between officials within each category and between categories. While 'co-ordination' suggests an active EU effort to reduce differences in outcomes, the term 'open' signals that it is up to national governments what lessons they learn and apply at home. The latter term is more important, in the absence of EU authority to compel national governments to adopt more similar programmes (de la Porte *et al.*, 2001: 296; Enterprise Directorate-General, 2002: 10ff.).

The European Commission has sought to formalize peer group review by promoting the open method of co-ordination (OMC) as a means of encouraging a European employment strategy. This has led not only to the compilation of detailed national reports about employment measures, but also to a system-atically designed series of visits of employment officials to other countries to compare their programmes. An evaluation of the process concluded that, while the visits produced an increase in specific knowledge about what other countries were doing, it did not lead to action (Casey and Gold, 2004). The occurrence of learning without action was due to the fact that the motive for travelling abroad was not to dispel domestic political dissatisfaction. It was to co-operate without commitment.

Since the programmes of a national government differ in kind from each other, a health policymaker will not turn to the department of defence for ideas about what to do, nor will military strategists seek advice from health specialists. Because the choice of countries for learning depends on the problem at hand, national policymakers adopt a 'horses for courses' strategy, looking to different countries and continents according to the issue. Within a national government, one department may look to Sweden for lessons about child care, to the United States for lessons about deregulation, and to Tony Blair's Britain for lessons in 'spin doctoring'. Where you look depends on where you are coming from and where you want to be in future.

Stage II
Venturing abroad

Step 4

Finding out how a programme really works there

When assessing the reliability and usefulness of information, officials tend to place the greatest reliance on their own senses – what they saw or heard, particularly informally and particularly from people or sources they trusted.

Harold Wolman and Edward C. Page, *Learning from the Experience of Others*

If you want to learn how a programme works, there is no substitute for seeing it in action. Studying laws, organization charts, budgets, and quantitative indicators of output are necessary but not sufficient. Within national politics, policymakers take for granted the desirability of talking to officials elsewhere about programmes of common interest. To understand how a foreign programme works, it is likewise necessary to talk to the foreigners who run the programme, for they not only write the documents that describe it but also know what those documents leave out. Investigating a programme on the ground shows how it looks from the inside. While a television feature may stimulate interest in foreign achievements, it is an inadequate basis for making policy. It is also far cheaper to send a government official abroad for a week than to send a television team abroad to produce a ten-minute segment for a public affairs programme.

When exchanging information about how programmes are working within a country, you talk with people you know and trust. However, policymakers embedded in a 'world' of face-to-face ties can find that others in their network have no better idea than they themselves do. The limitation of learning from others close at hand is even more evident in national government, because national officials spend most of their time dealing with others in the corridors of their own headquarters or with friends and enemies in agencies that are a walk or short taxi ride away. When there are strong domestic pressures to find a new programme, deciding whether to search among friends or strangers is less important than the choice between going somewhere or staying home.

When you turn to strangers in strange countries, communication is more difficult. Having friends in a foreign country is not necessary to collect basic information about programmes that are a matter of public record. But since most foreign governments work in a foreign language, this presents a challenge. Now that English has become the common language for communication between national governments on almost every continent, language barriers are much reduced for American and British policymakers. However, there remain cultural barriers to understanding documents about an unfamiliar country. What national policymakers say in a formal presentation to an international gathering may not be what they say when talking over a drink in their national capital.

Policymakers in national government have many opportunities to meet foreigners dealing with common problems since, as the next section shows, there are many forums in which programmes are discussed by officials from many countries and continents. In addition, there are informal forums in which officials can meet academics and experts outside government to discuss matters of common professional interest. Moreover, national professional associations usually encourage international meetings with counterparts from other countries. However, familiarity in talking to foreigners is no substitute for studying what they do at home. The second section of this chapter offers practical tips about preparing for travel and learning fast on the ground. The basic strategy of inquiry is: divide and learn.

Forums for learning: official and unofficial

In the contemporary world, governments of small and populous countries, and of poor as well as rich countries, have no difficulty in finding places where policymakers discuss problems of common concern, and something useful might be learned. The functional range of forums is vast too, for there are international institutions dealing with everything from the seabed to the weather and from international flows of money to international flows of fish.

Official forums bring together government policymakers within and across continents (Box 4.1). Geographical scope can be limited to neighbours, as in the North American Free Trade Agreement (NAFTA), or to a region, such as the European Union or the Asian Development Bank; or it can be global, as in the case of the United Nations. Functional forums concentrate on a limited set of issues of common concern. Specialized UN agencies such as the World Health Organization are both functional and global, whereas the European Central Bank's membership is confined to a minority of European countries. International agencies also exist outside the United Nations orbit; Interpol (the International Criminal Police Organization), for example, was founded in 1914 to link police departments across national boundaries in order to apprehend criminal networks operating across countries or continents.

Unofficial forums are usually networks of functional experts, since highway engineers and public health specialists in one country often have more to discuss

Box 4.1 Many official forums for crossnational learning

Examples of 118 intergovernmental organizations:

GLOBAL OR MULTI-CONTINENTAL IN SCOPE (30 organizations)

- United Nations, including specialized agencies such as the Food and Agricultural Organization and the International Labour Organization.
- International Monetary Fund, the World Trade Organization, the World Bank, and the Organisation for Economic Co-operation and Development (OECD).
- OPEC (the Organization of the Petroleum Exporting Countries).
- Commonwealth of countries formerly part of the British Empire.
- Commonwealth of Independent States formerly part of the Soviet Union.

EUROPE (39)

- European Union institutions in places scattered from Thessaloniki to Dublin include the European Commission, European Centre for the Development of Vocational Training, the Community Plant Variety Office.
- Agencies dealing with parts of Europe, such as the European Broadcasting Union, the Nordic Development Fund, the Danube Commission.

NORTH AND SOUTH AMERICA (16)

- Organization of American States, Central American Common Market, the Andean Community.

AFRICA (16)

- African Union, Common Market for Eastern and Southern Africa, the Niger Basin Authority.

ASIA/PACIFIC (9)

- Asian Development Bank, the Pacific Islands Forum.

MIDDLE EAST (8)

- League of Arab States, Gulf Cooperation Council.

Source: Turner, 2002, pp. v–viii.

with their professional counterparts in another country than with each other. Unofficial forums offer opportunities for national policymakers and their critics to exchange information with each other as well as with foreigners.

Forums for governments

Governments join intergovernmental organizations in the belief that they will gain from meeting representatives of other governments. The expected gains can include money, status, or knowledge. Knowledge about the programmes of other governments is usually a secondary motive or an incidental byproduct of participation in official international forums.

The United Nations was founded in 1945 with 50 member states and now has 189 members. Its size and diversity are both strengths and weaknesses. Diversity requires six official languages – Arabic, Chinese, English, French, Russian, and Spanish. Each of the five permanent members of the Security Council – China, France, Russia, the United Kingdom, and the United States – has veto powers. However, political power does not make the permanent members of the Security Council examples for countries seeking to learn how to improve public policies. In some instances – for example, the Russian Federation's half-transition to a market economy and democracy, or the corruption of the People's Republic of China – they offer lessons of what not to do.

The G8 group holds summit meetings of the heads of eight powerful countries from three continents, Britain, Canada, France, Germany, Italy, Japan, Russia and the United States. For this reason, their annual three-day meetings momentarily capture headlines. However, after allowing for press briefings, photo opportunities, and relaxation, the leaders have very limited time to consider a few topical issues. Moreover, the national leaders attending are usually more concerned with 'high' policy than with the nuts and bolts of programmes. A byproduct of the G8 summit is that there is a network of sherpas, high-ranking national officials who do the preparatory work for the summit meetings. They remain in contact throughout the year and can facilitate contacts between countries as and when there is a desire to learn about specific programmes.

International aid agencies give developing countries both money and advice tied to specific programmes and projects. Over the decades, organizations such as the World Bank have shifted from allocating money to build physical infrastructure such as highways and dams, to making grants to fund an increase in human capital through programmes for education, health, and the reduction of poverty. Since recipient countries often have inadequate programmes as well as inadequate funds for achieving these goals, the World Bank also gives technical assistance. In advising on programmes for developing countries, World Bank officials can draw lessons from experience in many developing countries as well as from the countries that provide most of the Bank's funds. The Bank annually prepares a *World Development Report* (2002a) that distils lessons about a major development problem, such as poverty or institutions of governance.

The International Monetary Fund's immediate priority is responding to national or international monetary crises by offering money and programme advice. When a government's national currency is in free fall in international money markets because of inflation and foreign debt, the IMF offers short-term loans to stabilize the currency. Its loans are tied to conditions: the receiving country is expected to cut public expenditure, reduce borrowing, and adopt pro-market programmes. The conditions are officially described as lessons learned from the experience of dealing with previous financial crises in other countries. For example, in a heavily indebted low-income country, 'We tell the government that if its inflation rate is 150 per cent and its interest rate is only 100 per cent, this can't go on indefinitely, for lenders will stop lending.' The Fund's conditions are known unofficially as the 'Washington consensus'; they emphasize free market practices reducing the role of the state. As well as fighting fires lit by monetary crises, the Fund tries to engage in fire prevention. It offers courses training national officials in the principles of the Washington consensus as well as in technicalities of public finance. It also conducts periodic reviews of all member governments to give warning of national programmes that it thinks could increase financial instability. However, until there is a crisis requiring a government to go to the IMF for an emergency loan, national policymakers can ignore its advice.

The Organisation for Economic Co-operation and Development (OECD) is a forum for ideas rather than a cash-dispensing machine. More than two dozen of the world's most developed nations on four continents use it to exchange information about social and economic programmes. Staff at OECD's Paris headquarters compile statistics that can be used to benchmark the performance of national programmes. Staff also prepare detailed reports that compare programmes associated with different outcomes. Every government has an official delegation to OECD that can provide contacts if it wants more information from that source. Government officials of member states regularly meet to compare programmes in their area of common concern. Frankness is encouraged by discussions being conducted outside the spotlight of world summits. Because the OECD does not distribute money, national representatives are free to take away from its meetings whatever lessons they deem useful.

The European Union is distinctive in that its forums make decisions that influence programmes in the EU's twenty-five member countries. The European Union's scope for policymaking covers a broad range of social, economic, and regulatory concerns of national government departments. The EU headquarters in Brussels has up to two dozen directorates specializing in different policy areas, and sources of proposals independent of national governments. Since the EU is concerned with detailed regulations, meetings of member states usually focus on narrow programmatic issues. In this way national officials learn about distinctive features of programmes of each national government. The cumulative effect is that most departments of national governments in Europe now have a number of officials who have learned a lot about programmes in other countries through participating in discussions at Brussels. They also have a network of contacts with counterparts in other countries that they can call on as and when appropriate.

Forums for knowledge and advocacy

While official forums are restricted to representatives of national governments, knowledge of public programmes is not. Unofficial forums complement official forums by disseminating knowledge free of the political constraints imposed by democratic governments and dictatorships, both of which are represented in international organizations such as the United Nations and the World Bank. Advocacy groups operating across national borders can advance ideas opposed to those of many national governments.

By definition, knowledge-based forums are specialized because expertise requires professional training and intensive commitment. Since scientific knowledge is not bounded by national frontiers, it is natural for experts in one country to make links with experts in other countries to transmit knowledge in the natural sciences, medical sciences, or social sciences (Haas, 1990). These knowledge-based communities often have formal international organizational links as well as professional ties. While such groups share knowledge, they often disagree about how governments should apply it. Economists are a striking example of professionals who dispute policy prescriptions by other economists in their field. Moreover, even though some members of these epistemic communities currently hold, formerly hold, or in future will hold posts in government, their knowledge does not give them the political authority and legitimacy to take controversial decisions.

Universities are a major extra-governmental source of expertise relevant to public policy. This is most evident in departments training people whose skills will lead to employment in the public sector, such as social work or public health, or to jobs in private sector organizations whose products are much influenced by public programmes, such as aeronautical engineering, genome research, or tax law. There is often a tension within academic departments and even within an individual professor between pure research, unconstrained by considerations of practical politics, and a desire to apply research in ways considered likely to make society better.

Senior civil servants, with or without a Ph.D., are often experts in the subject matter of the programmes that they administer as well as in the intricacies of public administration. In fields such as public health, highway engineering, or geodesic surveying, a professional qualification may be necessary to become a civil servant. In other fields, such as tax or social security administration, expertise can be learned on the job.

Knowledge-based forums in fields as diverse as primary education and nuclear physics bring together policy professionals in and out of government to discuss problems of common interest and concern, even though they may have different kinds of jobs and employers and may differ in their policy goals. In such forums, some participants are respected for their theoretical insights and others for their applied skills, while a small proportion combine both. In an era of increased occupational mobility, many participants are in-and-outers, having held positions within government and worked in universities or professional organizations independent of government.

Internationally active pressure groups are primarily concerned with advancing their members' material interests; learning is a byproduct of their advocacy role. For example, the World Tourism Organization was established in 1925 to promote tourism in the age of the steamship and steam train. Although the means of travel have changed and the volume of tourists has increased greatly, it still seeks to promote the interests of the tourist industry in many official forums, such as the European Union and international airline associations, as well as with national governments. Its membership brings together independent states, dependent territories, and private and public sector firms in the travel and tourist industry.

The members of most advocacy groups are non-governmental. For example, the International Confederation of Free Trade Unions consists of the peak national organization of trade unions, such as the British Trades Union Congress. The World Council of Churches includes more than 340 different organized Christian religions. Think tanks promoting ideas out of favour with their national government often turn to international networks in search of lessons that can be applied as and when they gain office. For example, national pressure groups seeking to promote privatization looked to Thatcherite think tanks in the 1980s, and before Tony Blair won office in Britain he looked to the third way strategy of Bill Clinton to develop a political rhetoric to win centrist voters.

Transnational campaign groups are concerned not so much with transmitting knowledge as with exercising political influence, for they know what they want done. Transparency International wants to reduce corruption in governments around the world, Oxfam is dedicated to promoting the cause of the poor, and Greenpeace wants to protect the environment. Campaign groups can make use of international benchmarking results in their effort to create dissatisfaction with the status quo. They can promote a successful national programme as a lesson from which other governments can learn. By contrast, advocacy groups with goals that have yet to be realized in any country are confined to offering speculative solutions to the problems that they diagnose.

Insofar as international forums are places to swap ideas rather than generate action, learning is the chief benefit of participation. A student seeking to write a term paper may be overwhelmed by the scale and variety of potential lessons discussed in an international forum. Busy policymakers are not. The diversity of programmes is an asset for policymakers because it offers a menu from which programmes that are inappropriate in terms of political values or resources required can be deleted, and a measure that is politically congenial and economically feasible might be identified (see Steps 7 and 8).

No substitute for going there

In international forums talking to people in the coffee break and random contacts at receptions can introduce you to strangers who know how their national programmes work and who can make them sound interesting, and on a university campus there are foreign students and faculty who can do likewise. While such serendipitous encounters can stimulate the imagination, they are no substitute for examining a programme on the ground.

Time and timing are of the essence and often in conflict. The more time there is to study abroad, the less immediate the need for what you learn. Thus, a student can spend more than a year abroad researching a thesis, whereas a public official under pressure to come up with a new programme in a few weeks cannot. When a problem facing government has a relatively long gestation period, there can be time for the government of the day to appoint a commission to investigate over a year or two, and travel to examine foreign examples. This is especially the case when a government does not want a report until after the next general election. An unusual example of learning from abroad occurred when the British government introduced the value-added tax, which was a condition of its entering the European Union. It was a prime necessity for the new tax to be immediately effective, but British officials had no experience of how it worked. Since a number of European countries were routinely administering such a tax, the British customs and excise staff visited European countries to learn at first hand what to do (and what not to do) to make the tax effective (Johnstone, 1975).

The more pressing the demand for new ideas, the less time there is to learn whether a programme with an international reputation would work if applied at home. If the purpose of a visit is symbolic, then a short stay is enough, and saves public money. For example, the British Commission on Electoral Reform, chaired by Lord Jenkins, devoted only a few days to examining the electoral systems of New Zealand and Australia. The critical knowledge that the commission required was not how foreign electoral systems worked, but how far the prime minister was prepared to countenance any change in the system that had produced a landslide majority to support him in Parliament.

Preparation

Before being parachuted into the midst of another national government, it is worthwhile investing at least a little time in preparation. The embassy of the host government can be asked to provide basic documents, such as the national constitution, and briefing documents about the government of the day. Since an embassy wants to cultivate contacts with a foreign government, it may also provide an instructive lunch. The World Wide Web now provides a cornucopia of practical information about national governments (www.gksoft.com/govt/en/). Buying a textbook on the political institutions of the country to be visited will provide much more information and the delays of air travel usually guarantee enough time to read it before the first meeting abroad. Doing so avoids wasting time by asking elementary questions or exposing your ignorance of the institutional framework of your host government.

A policymaker often starts a journey with two handicaps, ignorance of how the host government works and of its language, and with one big advantage, practical knowledge of a particular problem and programmes of concern to both countries. The latter is a very big advantage, since the purpose of a trip is not to develop linguistic skills or pass an examination in comparative politics, but to learn something useful to take home within a specific specialist field of public policy. Programmes addressing a common problem are likely to have similar concepts and similarities in technical terms. To draw lessons you do not need to be able to read novels and poetry of the host country's great writers. You do need, however, enough sensitivity to crossnational differences in institutions to avoid what the French call false friends, for example, thinking that an American state is the same as a European state; that a German *Land* is the equivalent of an American state; and that French *departements* are a part of Cabinet government rather than the ninety-six territorial units into which France is divided for nationwide administration.

Once on the ground in a foreign country, if you understand enough about programmes, you do not need a degree in a foreign language or in comparative politics to get the information that you need to take home. The skills required are akin to those of a good journalist: a capacity to know where to look; what questions to ask in order to extract information from strangers; and how to cross-check what one person tells you against what others say.

Divide and learn as a strategy of inquiry

Broad generalizations about what a country thinks about a programme are likely to collapse on arrival there, because every programme has a political dimension, and politics is about the expression of conflicting opinions. In addition to seeking the views of those officially responsible for what appears to be a success story, you should also seek the views of those who view the programme from other vantage points in order to learn what they may add or subtract. A simple name for the strategy is: divide and learn. If you ask people in different positions the same questions and their answers consistently support each other, this indicates a consensus that the programme is producing satisfaction. If criticisms are heard early in a stay, they can be used as the basis for subsequent questioning in order to test how much substance these criticisms have. To see a programme from different perspectives, talk to:

- *Politicians and officials taking the credit.* From the top of a government department, you can learn about the political interests supporting a programme; the claims it makes on political as well as tax resources; and emerging difficulties that policymakers think may require programme amendments or changes in the foreseeable future.
- *Foot soldiers of service delivery.* A national programme for education, health, or crime prevention looks different from the 'under all' position of a classroom teacher, a doctor, or a policeman. Those who deliver programmes see its effects immediately, both good and bad. Even the most satisfactory programme will have some shortcomings – and those delivering it are more likely to be conscious of defects than are high-level policymakers.
- *Experts and commentators.* University-based experts usually have a wealth of ideas and empirical data evaluating a programme's multiple consequences. The absence of official responsibility leaves experts free to criticize what government is doing, though it also allows them to dismiss practical constraints on action. Journalistic commentators know the personalities and politics associated with a programme, and what is important in 'selling' it to supporters.
- *Programme recipients.* When programmes target organizations (whether business associations or other agencies of government), the people to see can easily be identified. When a programme addresses specific categories of individuals, for example, disabled people or unemployed people, direct contacts are more difficult to organize but should be made. Sitting with even a few recipients is worthwhile, especially if you can think yourself into the position of those who are the object of a programme.
- *Reformers and critics.* A programme that produces satisfaction can nonetheless have shortcomings. The question to ask critics is whether they are demanding more resources to enhance the existing programme, or reforms to increase its effectiveness in reaching accepted goals; or whether critics want to replace an existing programme with another measure.

In the course of one business week, a visitor has time for five breakfasts, five lunches, and five dinners, as well as ten half-days for office interviews and on-site meetings. By the end of a week, intensive one-on-one and group discussions can be had with fifty or more people. If the people you meet are carefully selected to reflect different perspectives on the same programme, this is enough to give a rounded picture of its strengths and weaknesses. And such a schedule even allows time to shop for souvenirs at the airport on a Saturday morning trip home.

Tips for interviewing

Interviewing strangers is an art that requires common sense and concentration on the object at hand. Appearing from afar as an admirer of a national programme is likely to produce goodwill. But policymakers are busy, and to secure their time you must engage their interest by avoiding asking for information that can be garnered from standard reference sources. Instead, ask sympathetic yet thought-provoking questions. Self-effacement is also required: to learn, one must listen rather than provide gratuitous information about your own problems and country.

When interviewing a foreign policymaker, have a short list of topics and open-ended questions. The starting point of a semi-structured interview can be a general question that invites your host to say whatever he or she thinks you ought to know. Your host will want to get this out, and the sooner this is done the better you will be placed to probe for more details. This requires agility in phrasing questions that relate your interests to your host's interests and, on occasion, dragging your host back to topics of your concern. It also requires quickness in following up themes you had not expected and that are relevant to drawing a lesson. In an hour the original list of topics can be covered in any order that encourages a ready flow of meaningful answers – and new topics can be added.

After establishing a sense of rapport, questions can tactfully invite your host to admit mistakes, for example, asking what would be done differently if they were to launch the programme again from scratch. A sympathetic question about current difficulties and what can be done about them should also be asked, for the answer will throw light on potential defects and also show whether your host is being smug. To secure frank answers to potentially awkward questions an interviewer must demonstrate that answers will be treated in confidence. This is done by avoiding attributing by name comments made to you by others. Showing respect for the confidence of others will gain you the confidence of the person you are speaking to.

Different strokes for different folks is a maxim that applies abroad as well as at home. Deference is appropriate with senior policymakers who outrank you in a governmental hierarchy. At the other end of the ladder, service delivery staff may be flattered by a visit from a foreigner, especially if their own national headquarters often ignores them. The relationship with recipients of a programme will differ depending on whether they are articulate and cosmopolitan, for example, exporters, or relatively inarticulate or uneducated, as may be the case with unemployed people.

At the end of a day's fieldwork, look at your notes to see which points different sources agree on; which are disputed and why; and what points about the programme are still unclear and require further probing. Group discussions, whether around a table in an office or in a restaurant or pub, can be used to raise questions that invite several hosts to debate the answer with each other. In a complementary way, a quiet drink or meal with one individual who appears both knowledgeable and frank may elucidate confidences that would not be voiced in an official setting or in front of colleagues.

Near the end of a trip, you should spend a quiet evening interviewing yourself about what you have learned so far that can be used to draw a meaningful lesson. You can then put these tentative conclusions to your hosts to see whether or not they endorse what you have learned about their programme and what they think of the lesson that you will draw from their experience after returning home.

Step 5

Turning anecdotes into a model

Getting to the moon isn't the problem; it's getting back.
Astronauts' maxim

The simplest question that a policymaker faces after returning from travel abroad is, 'How was your trip?' The simplest answer is to tell a series of anecdotes about what happened, giving impressions of people, places, and colourful and unexpected incidents. Anecdotes reflect experience, and acquiring experience about the working of a programme in its national context is an essential step in lesson-drawing. But such anecdotes are about the experience of foreigners and, by definition, foreigners are different. For that reason, many policymakers will reject alien ideas without further thought.

The hardest question to answer is, 'What did you learn?' Learning is about turning experience into knowledge that can be applied at home. A policymaker wanting to bring useful knowledge back from abroad must be capable of abstracting something portable from that experience. In the world of politics, it is rare for generalizations to be totally fungible, that is, applicable any time and anywhere. The programmes of national governments are not as portable as laws of physics expressed in the universal language of mathematics. But this does not mean that what is learned from travel is necessarily confined to a single time and place.

The challenge facing a traveller is to identify the necessary features of a foreign programme in order to create a portable model that transcends its national context. Within the social sciences, economic theory is pre-eminent in making use of models to demonstrate with the clarity and precision of mathematics how any economic system could work. However, economic models cannot be used for lesson-drawing, because they are deduced from abstract principles rather than drawn from experience. Nor are economic models suitable for describing how an unfamiliar programme works, because they are not learning models, but are closed to the addition of observations outside (and often inconsistent with) the assumptions on which economic theories rest.

The education of doctors shows how models used for learning lessons can be applied in practice. Whereas a successful novelist describes distinctive characteristics of a particular individual in full-flesh detail, a medical student has a much bonier approach, studying models of the human body in skeletal form. No medical professor would ever claim that a skeleton displays what a person is actually like in the flesh. The object of an anatomy lesson is to demonstrate the normal structure of the human body, whatever the personality of the skeleton. Similarly, while the affairs of the heart in a novel will be suffused with personal detail, the model of a heart in a physiology textbook is totally impersonal. It concentrates on what is necessary for the flow of blood: the means by which blood enters the heart, its movement through the heart, and how blood is pumped into the body's circulatory system. The object of studying textbook models is to identify cases where individuals depart from the textbook norm in ways that cause ill health and to prescribe treatment that will give a patient better health.

A model is similar to the plan that a government department should draw up for major long-term projects such as the construction of a dam or airport. It shows in outline form what is needed to capture the flow of water in a dam or to enable planes to land and take off. A host of professionals, such as construction engineers and lawyers, then fill in details for areas of their responsibility. At this stage the model moves from being a generic description of a dam or airport to a plan of what is required to build a specific facility. Likewise, the implementation of a new social programme can start with a model of how it is intended to work, which can then be turned into a blueprint for what is required to be implemented – such mundane things as the appointment and training of public officials to administer the programme, writing regulations, and informing the target audience how to claim benefits. While the unintended consequences of a social programme may be numerous, without a planning model there is a risk that a new programme will never be implemented or that there will be confusion, waste, and frustration after it is launched (cf. Pressman and Wildavsky, 1973).

To be useful in lesson-drawing, a model must be abstracted from a programme actually in operation elsewhere, so that it can be related back to the context from which it is abstracted. To be useful to policymakers, it must leave out distracting details that are not necessary for its operation, details that confuse the distinction between what is interesting and what is essential. The first section of this chapter sets out how a model can be constructed from the observation of foreign programmes. The second section emphasizes what a model should leave out in order for it to be applied effectively after returning home.

What a model is

A model is a generic description of how a programme works. The purpose of making a model is to describe a programme in terms sufficiently general for it to be portable across national boundaries, yet sufficiently concrete so that policymakers in the country importing a model will be able to relate each of its parts to activities with which they are familiar.

The conceptual nature of a model is particularly important when working across national boundaries, for concepts such as money refer to a common phenomenon whether the currency in question is the dollar, the pound, or the euro. It is even more useful when working across languages, for the object is not to enlarge the foreign-language vocabulary of policymakers but to stimulate fresh thoughts about familiar problems. Generic labels concentrate attention on essentials, thus rejecting the assumption that everything about a programme is equally important. In lesson-drawing the critical feature of the British Inland Revenue or the American Internal Revenue Service is not that the offices of one display a picture of a queen while the other has the picture of a president, but that both are tax-collection agencies.

In addition to showing everything that is necessary to make a programme work, a lesson-drawing model must also leave out everything that is non-essential. Although each automobile engine has a unique serial number and each car a unique license number, the diagrams showing how to maintain and repair a car do not give the serial number of each engine. Diagrams of automobiles give generalized knowledge applicable to hundreds of thousands of cars with different engine numbers, colours, and license numbers, driven in many countries and continents.

Because a programme consists of a distinctive combination of the resources of government, the elements of a model are diverse. A model must specify the laws and regulations setting out what public agencies must or can do when operating a programme and what they cannot do. It must identify the organization or organizations responsible, the personnel, and the source of funding for a programme. It must also specify what the programme's outputs are to be – money, services, physical infrastructure, or regulations and inspection – and what sorts of individuals or organizations are the intended targets of a programme. A programme may have a single major goal or many goals. The fewer the goals, the easier it is to achieve success, since the outcome of a programme depends not only on the resources that it mobilizes but also on what individuals and organizations do independently of a specific programme (Box 5.1).

A model must be comprehensive in order to direct attention towards *all* the elements that are necessary for a programme to operate. It avoids jumping to the conclusion that a single 'quick-fix' action will be sufficient to achieve a programme goal. For example, lengthening the hours when people can vote should boost election turnout as long as all other conditions remain equal. But

---

Box 5.1 The elements of a model

To describe how a programme works, a model must identify:

- Laws and regulations: They specify the criteria for determining how outputs are to be produced and the conditions for being a recipient, whether the service is health care or imprisonment for a crime.
- Organization: Every programme must have one or more organizations responsible for producing outputs, whether they are in the public or the private sector.
- Personnel: Specialists, such as doctors delivering health care or air traffic controllers, and generalists, such as secretaries, computer programmers, and accountants.
- Money: Finance can come from general tax revenue, earmarked taxes, user charges, or a combination of sources.
- Programme outputs: They may be cash payments, services of public employees, or physical goods such as roads.
- Programme recipients: They may be individuals (mothers, students, consumers) or organizations (businesses, other government agencies, foreign countries).
- Goal: This is the outcome a programme is intended to promote, such as reading skills of poor children or low accident rates on the highway.

---

if this does not happen – there may be heavy rain on election day, or the weather may be good but all parties unpopular – this will tend to depress turnout. Models vary in their complexity. Keynes's model of economic activity can be reduced to a small number of equations as sparse as those of Einstein. By contrast, a computer model used to estimate national tax revenue can contain hundreds of variables, and a model of the international economy must include what happens inside a multiplicity of economies as well as the links between economies, steps that can require thousands of variables and tens of thousands of lines of computer code.

The fall of a dictatorship can be followed by demands for a free election in a country where such an event is unknown or unfamiliar, and the explosion of democracies in recent years has created a large number of not-for-profit organizations offering new democracies lessons in how to conduct free elections (see, for example, www.idea.int; Rose, 2000). This requires more than the enactment of laws, for an election is free and fair only if officials in charge of the process administer laws in accordance with recognized standards. In new democracies, failure to do so is as likely to reflect inexperience as partisan bias.

The role of foreign election advisors is to offer lessons from their own experience about how to administer each step in a free and fair election from the time the date of the ballot is decided to the declaration of winners and action

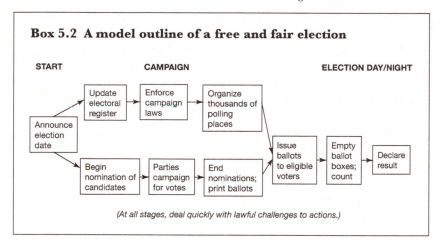

Box 5.2 A model outline of a free and fair election

START   CAMPAIGN   ELECTION DAY/NIGHT

(At all stages, deal quickly with lawful challenges to actions.)

on challenges from losers. Many of the steps shown in Box 5.2 may appear obvious to experienced election workers. The point of the model is to share this knowledge with officials who have never organized a free and fair election. The model can make clear to inexperienced officials what must be in place before election day. It also is an agenda for focusing the attention of officials in the countryside and cities on what must be done for voting to proceed without being marred by incompetence and fraud, and for the result to be accepted as accurate by losers as well as winners.

A model shows how a programme works by tracing the cause-and-effect links between its elements. A cake recipe is more than a list of ingredients; it is also a set of instructions about how the ingredients should be combined to make a cake. Similarly, a model should show how disparate parts of a programme are linked in order to produce its output. This makes a model different from a simple budgetary description of the amount of money and personnel required. A model traces how the agency responsible for a programme combines its inputs to produce outputs and deliver them to recipients. In medical terms, a model goes beyond anatomizing the bare bones of a programme; it also shows its physiology, that is, its vital processes in the body politic.

A cause-and-effect model of a programme makes it possible to simulate its effect by changing one or more of its elements. This is particularly desirable in lesson-drawing, because it is about considering what would happen if a programme were introduced in a new setting. With a cause-and-effect model, it is possible to simulate the consequences for voter turnout of holding an election on a weekend, when fewer people are at work, rather than on a weekday. In the United States computerized models are applied to census data to simulate the electoral outcome of different ways of drawing the boundaries of districts of members of Congress. Because public policy simulations depend on assumptions, their results are uncertain; medical models likewise deal in probabilities rather than certainties. When a doctor treats a specific patient, the treatment is based on a cause-and-effect model of the body – but medical knowledge is such that the best prognosis that can be offered is the likelihood that the treatment will be successful, but there always remains a possibility, whether 5 in 100 or in 1,000, that the outcome will be different from what is expected.

Military strategists are strongly committed to the use of models, for soldiers have few opportunities to fight wars. Surprise attacks allow little time for preparedness and the penalties for failure are great, and changes in technology and politics can make the experience of the previous war of limited relevance to the next. A distinctive feature of military strategy is that it requires an interactive model, since it is necessary to take an enemy's moves into account as well as one's own, just as chess players must think not only of their own moves but also of their opponent's response.

A model is analytic rather than prescriptive. To show how a programme works in another country is informative rather than decisive. If the goal of the programme is deemed desirable, then the model can be used to design a programme at home, but if the goal is undesirable, this will not happen (see Step 7). A model can also be used to understand failures. For example, air safety officials have a model of how an aeroplane ought to take off, fly, and land. When a plane crash occurs, inspectors visit the wreckage to examine the plane's surviving parts and retrieve the plane's black-box recording data about what was happening in the moments leading up to the crash. The information is used to identify the parts of the plane's operating system that failed – and to take actions that reduce the likelihood of another crash. In principle, learning from the failure of other countries is much easier than learning from one's own failures, because distance absolves observers from blame for what went wrong. However, elected politicians prefer to be associated with success, even if only vicariously, rather than failure.

A model is a not a lesson but a precondition for lesson-drawing. Without knowledge of how a foreign programme works, learning can only occur impressionistically – and impressions can be misleading, especially about countries with which a visitor is not familiar. The purpose of a model is clinical; it is designed to show how a programme works. While a contextually rich description of a foreign programme may make it appear attractive, it does not meet the requirement of lesson-drawing: showing how it works in terms sufficiently general to be applied in other places.

What a model leaves out

When a new programme is planned from scratch, the starting point is a blank piece of paper or an empty computer screen. There is nothing to see because nothing has happened yet. Policymakers must make use of their professional skills and imagination to describe how the new programme ought to operate once it is put into effect. By contrast, when a lesson is drawn from a programme in effect elsewhere, there is an example of how a programme can operate. Policymakers then face the problem of adapting it.

If a little knowledge is a dangerous thing, the same is true of too much knowledge. It means that you can't see the forest for the trees. A botanist does not produce a leaf-by-leaf description of every oak tree in a forest. Instead, a botanist follows the fourteenth-century principle of Occam's razor, providing a parsimonious description of leaves and trees rather than elaborating masses of non-essential descriptive detail. Likewise, policymakers should omit from models everything that roots it in a particular place. A diagram of how an automobile engine works does not tell us the history of the firm making it, what car workers feel about the machines they produce, or what they eat in their lunch break. It shows what is necessary to put a car in motion.

A model of a programme should use generic concepts that characterize functions without reference to specifics of place. A description of a programme that is thick with detail can convey its feel, but risks degenerating into a lengthy narrative that is just one damned thing after another. A thick description lacks the portability of a model stripped down to a programme's essentials. Moreover, the ability of a traveller to produce a model of a programme is a telling indicator of whether or not he or she gained a clear understanding of the essentials of its operation.

The use of generic concepts leaves out much that is highlighted in a media story about a programme. Media reporting of the putative success of a foreign programme can stimulate a desire to learn more but, since it is likely to dramatize personalities and political struggles, it is of little use for lesson-drawing. Moreover, journalists are inclined to identify success with the enactment of a bill by the legislature, and ignore what happens when it is implemented. Such is the speed with which media news moves that policymakers can claim to be emulating a successful programme elsewhere when that programme has yet to be implemented. For example, American politicians began promoting the British model of enterprise zones for economic development before the British Parliament had finished enacting enterprise zone legislation (Mossberger, 2000: 56). A much talked-about programme should be examined on the ground to understand the reality behind the hype.

A model of a programme concentrates on how it works now rather than its history. Historical studies start by explaining how a programme originated and evolved. The more compelling the historical narrative, the greater the difficulty in identifying which particular elements in a history are critical. Insofar as a history emphasizes the role of individual decisionmakers, this implies the vacuous lesson that the backing of a powerful personality is essential for the success of a programme. Insofar as a history emphasizes the importance a window of opportunity created by exceptional circumstances, the implied lesson – wait for an opportunity before acting – is vague and banal.

An abstract model leaves out all features of a culture that have no observable influence on a programme's output. By contrast, cultural studies are prone to emphasizing an undifferentiated label for an assemblage of values, norms, and practices that may *or* may not have causal relevance. Culture thus becomes an opaque label obscuring generic cause-and-effect elements of a programme.

A lesson-drawing model differs from statistical analyses. A regression analysis of a programme appears precise because it is expressed in numbers down to several decimal places. It can assess the net influence of a multiplicity of elements on a programme. But a regression analysis is not a model, for it does not specify the linkages that are central to a lesson-drawing model. Only after a cause-and-effect model is created can the statistics generated by regression analysis become useful as a means of indicating the relevant weight and impact of its elements.

Constructing a model concentrates attention on the object of a trip. It is not to admire or puzzle at what foreigners do or to become expert in their customs and language. The object is to understand how a programme of a foreign government works there in order to bring back knowledge that can serve as a prototype in developing a programme that can be effective in the country that you know best.

Stage III
Returning home

Step 6
Drawing a lesson

Design is the core of all professional training; it is the principal mark that distinguishes the professions from the sciences.

Herbert Simon, *The Sciences of the Artificial*

A model of a foreign programme is the starting, not the end, point of lesson-drawing. The object is to put foreign experience to use by applying at home what you have learned abroad. With a model in hand, the design of a new programme does not start from scratch. Instead of a blank sheet of paper on which to record speculations, there is an outline of how a programme produces a given result elsewhere. The object is not to photocopy that programme, but to make use of what you have learned abroad to create a programme that can be put into effect here.

Programmes are designed rather than given, and design is an art requiring skill and judgement. Designing a new programme is not like assembling a model aeroplane by carefully following every step in a diagram. A public programme has both 'hardware' features that are relatively easy to transfer because they are independent of place, such as methods for inoculating people against a new disease, and 'software' features that affect the implementation of a programme, such as methods that encourage people to come forward for inoculation (Rogers, 1995: 14).

As Herbert Simon emphasizes, design is a professional skill that differs from the scientist's concern with knowledge for its own sake. Professional education is about applying knowledge as well as about understanding basic principles. The latter can be learned in a seminar while the former is learned on the job. Professionals demonstrate their skills by diagnosing a particular problem and making recommendations for action. A civil engineer builds a bridge by combining scientific knowledge about stresses in metal structures and on-site test bores of a particular river bed and its banks. Policymaking is a profession, too. However, the large number of uncertainties in politics requires more judgement or guesswork than does the design of a bridge or an office building.

Lessons drawn from failure are easy to apply, because they can be stated as maxims about what you should *not* do. For example, a study of why a foreign government failed to cope with a flood may conclude: there were inadequate safeguards to guard against infrequent yet heavy torrents of rain; flood protection facilities were not properly maintained and inspected; and emergency police and fire services were not trained to put up emergency flood barriers. While these lessons appear obvious, they nonetheless remain important, and the example of foreign failure makes them more immediately convincing as stimuli for action. The limitation of drawing lessons from the failure of others is that it usually does not offer positive instruction about what should be done.

Learning lessons from successful programmes is more appealing but also more difficult, because a positive lesson must specify in detail how a model based on a programme elsewhere can be applied here. The first section of this chapter discusses a variety of ways in which lessons can be drawn, ranging from photocopying another country's programme through making a synthesis from two programmes, to using foreign examples for disciplined inspiration or selective imitation. The second section shows the need to be flexible in applying a model by examining the process of lesson-drawing within the European Union. The goal of the EU is to increase the integration of programmes between member states, but the European Commission in Brussels does not have the political authority to impose uniform programmes. Instead, it encourages member states to harmonize their programmes. The musical analogy is apt, for programmes can be harmonized by a variety of instruments.

Applying a model

Lesson-drawing is like reverse engineering, a procedure that manufacturers use when they want to copy a successful product created by a competitor. Reverse engineering involves taking apart a competitor's product in order to find out how it works and adapting it so that it can be marketed as one's own. When a new and popular computer device comes on the market, for example, competitors buy it in order to find out how it works. This knowledge is summarized in a model. The next step is to design a product that the second manufacturer can produce. Because of patent and copyright law, the resulting product cannot be an exact copy of another's product. Yet alterations cannot be introduced arbitrarily; otherwise, the newly designed product may not work as intended or may lack sales appeal. The speed with which a new product is matched by 'copycat' products from competitors is evidence of rapid learning by firms marketing everything from computers to clothes.

Applying a model of a public programme is both easier and harder than the reverse engineering of fashion goods or a new electronic device. It is easier because public programmes are not copyrighted, and policymakers will regard it as giving them prestige if other countries want to copy what they do.

Moreover, the model abstracted from another government is usually fairly general; it therefore allows wide scope for choice when it comes to filling in the details of the programme based on it. For example, a model of free elections can leave open whether a national parliament is elected by proportional representation or by the Anglo-American first-past-the-post method. Yet the openness of a programme model creates difficulties insofar as it leaves out many practical details. Confronted with a foreign prototype, national policymakers are forced to find institutions in their own country that are functionally equivalent to those in the country of origin.

The extent to which policymakers stay close to the original when drawing a lesson is a matter of constitutional frameworks and political power. In a unitary state the discretion of local and regional authorities is much more limited than in a federal system, for a department in the national capital can impose a 'cookie cutter' model that stamps out virtually the same programme in every town hall. However, a national government cannot have a programme from another country imposed on it, as is often the fate of local government. Furthermore, when policymakers are under pressure to act, there is a wide choice of alternative programmes from which to draw lessons. The practical issue in lesson-drawing is whether the design of a programme draws on a single foreign example or a combination of foreign examples (Box 6.1).

Box 6.1 Alternative ways of drawing a lesson

- **Photocopying** — Producing an exact photocopy with a minimum of change in the names of institutions and places and dates.
- **Copying** — Duplicating almost all the elements of a programme already in effect in another place.
- **Adaptation** — Altering details of the design of a programme elsewhere without removing major elements.
- **Hybrid** — Combining elements of programmes with the same objective in different jurisdictions.
- **Synthesis** — Combining in a novel way familiar elements of programmes with the same objective.
- **Disciplined inspiration** — Responding to the stimulus of a programme's inspiration elsewhere by creating a novel programme not inconsistent with foreign examples.
- **Selective imitation** — Adopting attractive, but not necessarily essential, imitation parts of other programmes while leaving out awkward but essential bits.

Single examples

A programme is a *photocopy* of what is done elsewhere if the only differences between the original and the new measure are due to crossing out a few place names and dates specific to the original and inserting new ones. In a centralized state, the national government can lay down uniform standards that local governments must comply with in order to avoid challenge in the courts. For example, the administration of parliamentary elections is in the hands of British local authorities, but the rules governing election administration are laid down in Whitehall by central government. In such a situation, most modifications of the central programme are limited to filling in blanks with local addresses of the places where votes can be cast on election day.

Yet just as a poem translated from English into French or German cannot be the same as the original, so a programme that is translated from one country to another cannot be exactly the same. Even if the original source and the lesson drawn are both in English, that does not make the two programmes identical; the political institutions of Britain are not the same as the United States, nor are the federal institutions of Canada the same as those of the United States or Australia. However, the translation of a programme ought to be faithful to the original from which it is drawn.

Copying a programme by duplicating the great majority of its features establishes a single programme as a prototype while allowing for variation in minor details in order to allow for differences in context and in preferences of those doing the copying. Within a country copying is facilitated by a common framework of national laws and institutions. In federal systems copying a prototype recognizes that state and local authorities have a degree of discretion that is denied when a central design must be photocopied. In the United States the National Conference of Commissioners on Uniform State Laws drafts model legislation for programmes ranging from alcoholism to unclaimed property. Its efforts have led dozens of American states to copy more than 100 model laws in such fields as the commercial code and family law (Council of State Governments, 1990: 405ff.).

Copying is more difficult across national boundaries. In academic theories, national governments can be treated as no more than intervening variables in the globalization of health, education, and other social welfare programmes. But when programmes are moved across national boundaries, it is necessary to make alterations to take into account differences in language, legal procedures, institutions, and resources. If the political rationale is strong, a programme can be copied with very few modifications. For example, the electoral system enacted by the British government for use in Northern Ireland elections is the single transferable vote system copied from the Irish Republic rather than the standard British system.

Whereas a model is created by removing details of how a programme operates in the country of origin, applying a model across national boundaries requires the insertion of details about laws, institutions, and administrative procedures. *Adaptation* involves two governments in the one-to-one relationship of a leader and a follower. For example, the collapse of the Communist government of East Germany after the fall of the Berlin Wall in 1989 voided many of its Soviet-inspired programmes. The integration of the five East German *Länder* into the Federal Republic of Germany created a new constitutional framework within which East German *Länder* could adapt programmes consistent with federal legislation already in effect in West Germany (cf. Pickel, 1997; Jacoby, 2000).

One lesson with multiple sources

If two or more foreign programmes are observed, then a lesson can be drawn that is a *hybrid*, combining compatible elements of several programmes. All the elements of a hybrid programme can be observed in action, albeit in different places. When the Federal Republic of Germany was debating its electoral system, there were disputes between those who argued for choosing members of parliament by proportional representation, the normal practice of most continental European countries, and proponents of the Anglo-American first-past-the-post system. The upshot was a hybrid electoral system, in which half the members of the German Bundestag are elected by proportional representation and half by a first-past-the-post ballot. Forty years later, when post-Communist countries of Eastern Europe were choosing an electoral system, several adapted the German hybrid.

A lesson can be a *synthesis* if it combines elements from similar programmes in different countries in a distinctive way or if it combines foreign examples with elements of its existing domestic programmes. While the electoral system of a new democracy may be a unique synthesis of elements, each of its parts can usually be found in other free and fair electoral systems. When the need arose in post-Communist Europe to produce electoral laws fast, policymakers did not try to innovate. Instead, new laws synthesized elements from programmes in place in other countries. At times, elements were retained from the Communist past, for example, the requirement of at least a minimum turnout to make an election valid. A synthesis is particularly likely to emerge as the compromise outcome of a detailed process of bargaining. For example, the Hungarian electoral system is a synthesis. It mixes proportional representation and single-member districts in a manner adapted from Germany; it allocates proportional representation seats at two tiers along Scandinavian lines; and some members of parliament are elected from single-member districts with provision for two rounds of competition, as in France.

Foreign travel can open the eyes of policymakers to the fact that their own way of dealing with a problem is not the only way. When a foreign example appears more successful, it can inspire fresh thoughts. Senior politicians can return from a trip abroad or, in one British case, from a trip to the dentist inspired by what they have learned from a chance encounter. The task of investigating whether an attractive idea can be implemented is then delegated to expert officials, and the mode of lesson-drawing shifts from inspiration to perspiration. This is likely to require adding major elements that are different from the original source of inspiration. Yet since such a lesson will still have elements found in programmes elsewhere, it is not purely speculative. The outcome can be described as a work of *disciplined inspiration*, in which the original model, based on foreign examples, is the starting point for a series of modifications that go beyond simple adaptation.

Without the discipline of a model, attempts at lesson-drawing are no better than *selective imitation*. Imitation is selective when a lesson concentrates on those parts of a foreign programme that are congenial to policymakers while leaving out the hard parts that impose political costs. In such instances, policymakers do not want a model showing in detail how a foreign programme works; instead, they will 'cherry-pick' a few features of a programme that are appealing and incorporate these in a programme that is designed independently of foreign examples. When a foreign programme is associated with success, then imitating a few prominent features can also be used to legitimate what national policymakers design for their own purposes. For example, in the 1980s the privatization of public enterprises and assets became politically attractive to many governments. However, crossnational differences in political interests meant that some policymakers did not engage in systematic study of leading examples from Thatcher's Britain and Reagan's American programmes. Instead, they relied more 'on anecdote rather than evidence, a sign that legitimation rather than learning may be the motivating force' (Henig *et al.*, 1988: 459).

Applying lessons in the European Union

The European Union is distinctive in having substantial political resources to encourage lesson-drawing as part of its goal of creating a closer union of twenty-five member states with more than 400 million citizens. International treaties give it a measure of supranational authority over national governments and the European Court of Justice has the power to enforce treaty obligations. The European Commission in Brussels has up to two dozen directorates to promote, promulgate, and evaluate programme regulations, in consultation with the multinational popularly elected European Parliament and the European Council of Ministers, representing national governments. It also promotes programmes enabling young people to study and learn abroad in other member states. The Single Europe Market gives the European Commission a charter to issue regulations imposing common standards for programmes in order to ensure that national governments do not adopt programmes that would be barriers to the free movement of goods and services within the European Union.

However, the doctrine of subsidiarity, officially endorsed in the 1992 Treaty of Maastricht, appears to limit the capacity of Brussels-based institutions to impose programmes on member states. The doctrine holds that 'decisions are to be taken as close as possible to the citizen'. However, the treaty balances this decentralist principle by also stating that the EU can act 'if and insofar as the objectives of the proposed action cannot be sufficiently achieved by the member states'. The official explanation of the treaty definition of subsidiarity has been described by a former president of the European Court of Justice as 'a disgraceful piece of sloppy draftsmanship, so bad that one is forced to assume it must be deliberate' (quoted in Rose, 1996: 263).

The issues facing the European Union invariably involve political disagreements about what the standards and form of its programme ought to be. While European Union staff are pledged to take a supranational view of their work, they cannot neglect the political priorities and voices of its twenty-five member states. Decisions require endorsement by the national governments meeting in the Council of Ministers, and major decisions require unanimous consent. Because a large number of diverse national governments are required to endorse a proposal, this often leads to compromises or the adoption of standards that reflect the lowest common denominator of what national governments are already doing, rather than constituting benchmarking standards that push national governments to learn what other member states are doing and adapt their programmes accordingly.

A trickle-down and a trickle-up learning process

The authority of the European Union is exerted through a trickle-down process from its supranational institutions. But these institutions are subject to a steady trickle-up influence from member states and trickle-in influence from pressure groups that lobby at both the national and European levels (Cowles *et al.*, 2003). In more than two dozen European countries, national policymakers now have to learn Euro-speak, the mixture of English words and French ideas that constitutes the normal language of discourse in the European Union's headquarters in Brussels. Simultaneously, national policymakers exert pressure on officials of the EU's executive branch, the European Commission, to learn about their national programmes before it pronounces a European standard.

The adoption of the euro as the single currency of twelve member states of the European Union is an extreme example of a uniform programme. It came about after the failure of efforts to harmonize the exchange rates of national currencies among the central banks of EU member states. In place of the complexities of co-ordinating economic measures taken by central banks from Finland and Ireland to Portugal and Greece, the European Central Bank (ECB) in Frankfurt now sets interest rates and issues the currency for most citizens of the European Union. The ECB drew on the model of the German Bundesbank, because it had a successful anti-inflation record. While the ECB has been successful in keeping inflation down, its success has been limited. In particular, it has spectacularly lacked the political clout to impose sanctions on France and Germany, its two largest member states, when they broke ECB rules placing a ceiling on the size of a government's deficit.

At the other extreme, the principle of mutual recognition allows every member state to maintain a national programme intact without regard to programmes of other governments in the same field. Mutual recognition accepts that whatever meets the laws and standards of one member state must be accepted by all the other countries of the European Union, unless there is a clear threat to public health. The standard of mutual recognition was first enunciated by the European Court of Justice in the *Cassis de Dijon* judgment of 1979 and has subsequently been extended by political negotiations. Where the principle applies, it prevents the Commission from forcing national governments to alter their programmes to meet a Brussels standard (Nugent, 1994: 275). However, insofar as a national programme is inferior to that of other programmes in the EU, there remain economic pressures to learn from competitors how to improve it.

EU policymakers use the doctrine of harmonization in an effort to reconcile uniformity, which allows no scope for learning from other countries, and mutual recognition, which exerts no pressure to pay attention to what other member states are doing. Just as the notes that make up a chord on the piano are not the same, so EU standards recognize that harmony can be achieved by programmes that differ in significant elements. In the initial Treaty of Rome, harmonization was referred to as the approximation of programmes. This can be achieved if all national programmes in a given field meet common standards, for example, about safety in food processing or in factories. Setting common standards makes national governments take notice of the programmes of member states. This generates a pool of knowledge that each country's policymakers can draw on when there is pressure to introduce a new programme. More than that, harmonization implies a continuing pressure on programmes to conform to EU standards or to reduce differences between their programmes.

While treaties give lawful authority to the supranational European Union, the power to implement EU programmes remains with national governments. The largest bloc of officials in the European Commission are not policymakers but translators concerned with converting directives drafted in French or English into one or another of more than a score of languages of its member states. However, the people who translate the directives into national laws reside in twenty-five different capitals and they have substantial discretion in what they draw from EU regulations to make them in harmony with existing national practices. For example, both Britain and Sweden have the same obligation to implement an EU programme to consult with their local and regional governments when allocating money for regional aid. Each government does so in harmony with its pre-existing national practices. In the case of Sweden, this is also in harmony with the intent and spirit of Brussels; in the case of Britain, it is not (Box 6.2).

The *acquis communautaire* principle strengthens the top-down authority of the European Union. It states that once a grant of powers and responsibilities has been made to the EU by national governments, these powers cannot be taken back by the latter. It also binds member states to endorse additional programmes that are needed to implement existing EU powers, and the Maastricht Treaty contains an explicit commitment to use the *acquis* to this end. The many agreements that constitute the *acquis* normally set out rules and guidelines that all member states must follow; they do not mandate a uniform programme that

---

Box 6.2 Alternative ways of adapting a European Union programme

Structural programmes to promote the development of economically backward regions account for more than one-quarter of the expenditure of the European Union. Initially, the money was allocated by national governments in harmony with EU standards. But this led to protests from the regions that national governments were not following EU guidelines but using money from Brussels for other purposes. In response, the Commission decreed that within a country structural funds should be allocated by a partnership between central government and local, regional, and related authorities.

Established national practices for funding regional development differ substantially between the most and least centralized EU member states. For example, in Britain there is no regional tier of government and local government's spending powers are strictly controlled by the central Treasury Department. By contrast, in Sweden local governments have more financial autonomy; consultation between national and subcentral agencies is normal; the transparency of consultation is supported by freedom-of-information acts; and there is much more support for government leadership in economic development than in market-oriented Britain.

The partnership programmes that Britain and Sweden have adopted differ substantially. In Britain the central government's distrust of local authorities has been institutionalized by a high degree of Treasury control of their expenditure. Initially, civil servants rather than elected councillors represented the regions in consultations about the allocation of EU structural funds within the English regions, and they remain important. By contrast, in Sweden co-operation has long been the norm between multiple tiers of government and between elected representatives and corporatist representatives of trade unions and business. Thus, the Swedish government met EU requirements for consultation in allocating structural funds by mobilizing pre-existing networks of consultation.

Source: Bache and Olsson, 2001.

all member states must adopt. Since each agreement must be negotiated between existing member states, its terms are likely to be consistent with a variety of national programmes. While the *acquis* does not detail what a national government must do in programmatic detail, it provides a strong incentive for a national government to watch what others are doing in a given policy area.

The impact of the *acquis communautaire* is potentially greatest on countries that apply for membership in the European Union. As a condition of admission, applicant countries must accept EU programmes that are already in place. Most of the lengthy process of discussion between Brussels officials and applicant governments focuses on the former teaching the latter what modifications in their programmes may be required to harmonize with EU practices, a pressure that forces the applicants not only to examine their own programmes but also to look to existing member states for examples of programmes that are acceptable to Brussels.

The application of ten post-Communist countries to join the European Union offered an extraordinary opportunity for lesson-drawing, since all were adopting new programmes to replace Soviet-era measures. By the time discussions began, the *acquis* required more than 80,000 pages to set out. From 1997 onwards, the European Commission's PHARE programme allocated more than a billion euros to help applicant countries adapt their programmes in order to become eligible for membership. To promote lesson-drawing, the Commission sponsored 'twinning' arrangements in which officials from a ministry in one EU member state were seconded as pre-accession advisors to a similar ministry in an applicant country. In many cases, twinning arrangements lacked any underlying logic or were a reflection of interests of existing member states (Grabbe, 2002: 258ff.). For example, the Austrian ministry responsible for one of the most regulated labour market programmes in Europe was linked with Bulgaria to explain in English to Bulgarians how they could introduce market-oriented programmes in order to become economically competitive in the single European market.

In response to top-down pressure, Central and East European governments learned the lesson of existing member states, namely, to exert pressure on Brussels to accept their programmes and proposals for change as being in harmony with the *acquis*. There was not the technical or linguistic expertise in Brussels to go over all the fields covered by existing European Union programmes. Differences in programmes among established member states gave the applicant countries scope for identifying their own measures with programmes already accepted as being in harmony with the relatively abstract language of Brussels measures. Furthermore, there were very strong political pressures on EU negotiating officials to hasten the entrance of post-Communist countries to the European Union. Once applicant states understood the politics of enlargement, eight countries were able to draw lessons in accordance with domestic political imperatives and gain admission to the European Union (Jacoby, 2001: 188).

Altogether, the formulation of programmes in many areas of concern to twenty-five national governments of Europe is no longer totally introverted, as it can be in Washington. When a member government is planning a new programme, in addition to customary calculations of national politics, it must also consider whether EU rules and regulations are applicable. When a programme is already mutually recognized or in harmony with EU standards, the influence of Europe is exerted by the addition of ideas and information about programmes elsewhere. If a national programme is not up to standard or, more likely, if proposals emanate from the European Commission to alter EU regulations, the national officials are stimulated to look afresh at their own programme and at what other member states are doing in order to identify what changes Brussels might make that it would support and which it would oppose (Knill, 2001). Even if EU programmes have no direct relevance, policymakers can draw on the information and knowledge they gain from frequent contacts with their counterparts in other countries to evaluate national programmes, and, even if they do not do so, critics can cite examples of programmes elsewhere as examples of practices from which the government of the day ought to learn a lesson.

Step 7
Should a lesson be adopted?

This paper frightens me to death. We should recognise that the German talking shop works because it consists of Germans.

Margaret Thatcher, unpublished comment on a memo
about a German corporatist economic programme

Politicians are more concerned with political values than with the technical details of programmes. Therefore, the critical question about a proposed programme is: should it be adopted? Whereas drawing a lesson is about getting to grips with technicalities of programmes in two different countries, the adoption of a lesson is an exercise in political judgement. In a democracy, elected officials have the legitimate right to decide which values should be applied to evaluate a programme. In order to win endorsement, a lesson's values ought to be congenial, or at least not opposed to those of the governors of the day. This point is often ignored by proponents of best practice, who believe it is self-evident that whatever programme is identified as best by international comparison ought to be adopted without opposition.

The high-level civil servants and experts who advise elected policymakers have political as well as professional values. In the United States and most of Europe, the government of the day appoints advisors who share their political values. There is an ample supply of right-of-centre economists who favour measures to promote the market through privatization and deregulation, and an ample supply of left-of-centre economists who favour government intervention to help the poor and promote income equality. Civil servants can also evaluate programmes according to technical values, favouring programmes that are easy to implement and administer. Experts sometimes define policy goals in terms far narrower than those that appeal to politicians. For example, a World Bank (2002b: xix) review of the transition process of post-Communist countries did not define its goal as the consolidation of democracy. Instead, it offered as 'a natural definition of the end of transition' the closure of the productivity gap between formerly state-owned enterprises and restructured and new enterprises.

The adoption of any programme is a political process involving differences of opinion about what should be done and bargaining to arrive at an agreement. Critics can demand major modifications of a proposed lesson or even changes that sacrifice effectiveness as the price of their political support. If differences cannot be reconciled, then the lesson will not be taken off the drawing board and put into effect.

Because political values are disputed, they are potentially unstable. Even if the government of the day has a big majority in the legislature, its hold on office is secure only until the next general election. In addition, the priority given to competing values is subject to change with events. Whereas Americans had little concern with anti-terrorist programmes prior to September 11, 2001, since then homeland security has been a key criterion for assessing both domestic and international policies. Even bigger changes can be observed in China. A generation ago Chinese Communist leaders looked to Moscow for inspiration and programmes to build a socialist economy. Today, Beijing looks to the West for programmes, because it has abandoned Marxist values and now gives highest priority to building a market economy.

The comparative analysis of programmes within a well-established field of public policy will tend to convey widespread consensus if there is national satisfaction with programmes. However, this leaves out the origins of the programmes that today give satisfaction. Their initial adoption often occurred after bloody political battles. The way that these early battles were resolved is an important factor in accounting for differences between national programmes today. And the existence of unresolved battles is important in explaining why many proffered lessons are not, or not yet, adopted.

The first section of this chapter distinguishes between conflicts about the ends of programmes and the means used to achieve these ends. Elected politicians are likely to give more attention to debating programme goals, while experts are more likely to focus on programme means. Given value conflicts, the next issue that must be faced is: who decides? Just as the preparation of a lesson involves crossnational learning, so too national governments are subject to crossnational political pressures. The second section examines the mobilization of support *and* opposition to a lesson across national boundaries. The concluding section considers conditions in which political opposition to a lesson can change, thus encouraging the adoption of a measure that was once rejected as not wanted here.

Political conflicts about ends and means

Since politics involves conflicting opinions about what government ought to do, any lesson of political interest will face challenges about its ends or its means, or on both counts. The only way in which a lesson can avoid becoming subject to debate is by addressing issues of no political consequence. Confronted with a controversial issue, politicians can respond by proclaiming consensual goals such as peace and prosperity. While such goals are widely accepted, this does not mean the end of politics. It simply shifts debate to questions of means, for example, whether amending an existing national programme is likely to be more effective in promoting prosperity than introducing a new programme based on a lesson from abroad.

Values and value conflict

Theories of political culture emphasize the distinctiveness of national political values, and imply that trying to draw lessons across national boundaries will fail. The success of a programme in a given country is ascribed to its distinctive values and beliefs or 'style' of policy, implying that any attempt to export it elsewhere would be doomed to failure because each national culture is deemed unique. A programme that would be acceptable in Swedish political culture may not be acceptable in the United States, and vice versa. However, such general statements do not identify the specific features of a culture that are obstacles to lesson-drawing.

Generalizations about culture impute the same values to virtually every citizen of a country. From this perspective, Swedish programmes permitting abortion on demand will be rejected by Polish and Irish governments that do not want to challenge traditional anti-abortion norms in their societies. Yet election results serve as a reminder that there are differences of opinion in every democracy.

National politics usually involves value conflicts within a society. For example, a lesson recommending action to improve the environment by reducing automobile use will reveal differences in values between citizens committed to 'green' values and convinced motorists. Rejection of a lesson can be ascribed to cultural conflicts only if the values causing rejection are widely endorsed by all major political groups and are in conflict with values widely held in other countries, for example, because they originate in different religions.

The cultural values described as obstacles to adopting a lesson often divide a country. Crossnational public opinion studies document in great detail the extent to which there are major differences of opinion within every country on issues of high political salience, and crossnational similarities in the way in which national populations divide. For example, when the World Values Survey asks people in Europe and the United States about the priority they give material growth in the economy as against greater individual influence on work and community affairs, no national population is homogeneous. In every country, citizens disagree with each other (Box 7.1). About half of Americans, Britons, French, and Swedes favour economic growth, while one-third put participative values first, and one-sixth endorse other values offered. An incidental consequence of within-country differences of opinion is that there

Box 7.1 Values differ within as well as between countries

Q. There is a lot of talk these days about what the aims of this country should be for the next ten years. What would you consider most important?

	USA %	BRITAIN %	FRANCE %	SWEDEN %	Avg %
Economic growth	54	43	52	51	50
People have more say about work, community	26	40	36	33	34
Other	20	17	12	16	16

Source: Inglehart *et al.*, 1998, Variable 257.

are similarities in values across national boundaries. In European countries, as in the United States, some citizens give priority to economic growth while others do not.

Values can be used as a political fig leaf to cover up naked partisan interests opposed to a lesson. This is very evident when there is a debate about reforming the electoral system, which is central both to democratic values and to the political interests of elected officeholders. There is a vast political science literature about the relative merits of the Anglo-American first-past-the-post method of electing representatives and proportional representation systems used in most democratic countries. Administratively, there is no obstacle to substituting proportional representation for a first-past-the-post electoral system or vice versa. Moreover, once a ballot reform is introduced, there is no difficulty in securing the co-operation of political parties, for they must conform to the new system or lose by default through failing to qualify for a place on the ballot.

The interests of parties and politicians are critical in deciding whether or not an electoral system is changed. Proportional representation was introduced early in the twentieth century in many European countries, as ruling elites believed it would assure them seats in parliament after the introduction of universal male suffrage reduced their numerical significance in the electorate. In Britain, the electoral system was not changed because the Conservative and Labour Parties alternated in government, with the electoral system manufacturing a majority of seats for whichever party won a plurality of the popular vote. When the decline in the Labour Party vote in the 1970s and 1980s threatened it with permanent exclusion from power, Labour politicians showed an interest in proportional representation (Box 7.2). However, the 1997 election manufactured a landslide majority for Labour in Parliament even though it won little

Box 7.2 Political values as a cover-up for political interests

The Labour and Conservative Parties for many years were confident that each would alternatively enjoy a monopoly of government office as the first-past-the-post system manufactured a parliamentary majority for a party with a minority of the vote. Both parties therefore defended that electoral system. For the same reason Liberals favoured proportional representation, since the Liberal Party won disproportionately few seats compared to its share of the popular vote.

During eighteen years of Conservative government after 1979, many Labour MPs became attracted to proportional representation. They saw it as a means of ending the monopoly of power that enabled the government of Margaret Thatcher to put through a radical economic programme even though her party averaged less than 43 per cent of the popular vote in winning three straight elections, while the majority of the vote was divided between the Labour Party and the Liberal Democrats, and it appeared neither could be confident of winning a majority of seats in Parliament. On becoming Labour leader in opposition in 1994, Tony Blair began discussions with the Liberal Democrats about forming a coalition government. The Liberals made endorsement of proportional representation a condition of joining a Labour-led coalition and Blair expressed a willingness to consider proportional representation in return for their support for his becoming prime minister.

However, in 1997 Labour's political interests reversed, as it won 63 per cent of the House of Commons seats with 43 per cent of the popular vote. The introduction of proportional representation would destroy the Blair government's monopoly of power. Tony Blair lived up to his pre-election commitment to consider the subject by appointing a Commission on Voting Reform under Lord Jenkins. By doing nothing after the Commission reported, the prime minister protected the interest of the Labour government.

more than two-fifths of the popular vote. The Labour government therefore did not introduce proportional representation.

People learn but organizations decide

Political relevance guarantees that proponents of a lesson will face opposition from within government by those with an interest in the status quo. Any new programme invariably imposes costs, such as changes in personnel, abolishing a government agency, or increasing benefits to some groups but not others. Defenders of the status quo can argue that the costs of a new programme are real, while its benefits are hypothetical.

The idea of government as a body with a single mind does not accurately describe the network of organizations that become involved when a decision is to be made about adopting a lesson. A more apt metaphor is that of an octopus with eight arms, or a squadron of octopuses, some with the standard number of arms and others with a surprisingly indeterminate number of arms wanting to get into the decisionmaking act. The variety of organizations creates multiple opportunities for finding a sponsor for adopting a lesson; it also ensures the existence of multiple critics.

Within the field of government, a lesson is subject to scrutiny through the eyes of many different agencies. It will be examined carefully by the department that will be responsible for administering it; by departments whose existing programmes will be affected by a new measure; by officials controlling public expenditure; and by lawyers checking to be sure that the proposed programme does not violate existing laws. Before making a judgement about the attractiveness of a proposal, officials will consult with regional and local organizations responsible for administering a decentralized programme and with affected interest groups and experts.

Even when government is in the hands of a single party, this does not guarantee a single point of view. Elected decisionmakers are more concerned with electoral consequences and the impact of a lesson on their own political career than are professional experts who draw lessons. Departments tend to differ in the criteria they apply when evaluating a programme. For example, the treasury will be against proposals that threaten an increase in taxation, while education and defence departments tend to favour programmes that will increase public expenditure. In Washington the division of power between the White House and Congress institutionalizes conflicting opinions and interests. In the words of a Washington aphorism, 'Where you stand depends on where you sit.'

When a lesson must run the gauntlet of a multiplicity of organizations applying different values, the price of consent can turn a carefully modelled measure consistent with the experience of one other country into a hybrid that takes account of multiple political values or a political compromise that is the product of undisciplined inspiration.

Pressures from abroad

Any programme based on a foreign example necessarily involves contact between at least two countries, one providing a model and the other wanting to apply a lesson. In a world of intermestic policy concerns and a multiplicity of international institutions, every national government is involved in an ongoing exchange of influence, in which some national governments are more influential than others.

Compulsory lessons?

To assume that best-practice programmes sell themselves is naive. It ignores the dimension of power in international relations. Yet to claim that lesson-drawing can involve 'direct coercive transfer' (Dolowitz and Marsh, 1996: 347) is also naive, for it ignores tactics that poor governments can use to resist domination by strong and rich governments and intergovernmental institutions.

Whether a lesson is adopted or not is the result of the interaction between pressures at home, pressures from abroad, and the response of the government. The pressures to adopt or reject a lesson can be mutually reinforcing or in conflict (Box 7.3). When foreign pressure favours a programme deemed desirable by a country's government – for example, a World Health Organization recommendation to a low-income tropical country to adopt a programme to combat a tropical disease – adoption can be a process of co-operation. Reciprocally, if a programme is internationally recognized as a disaster, then national governors will want to avoid it and foreign advisors will not press for its adoption. It is logically possible for a national government to want to apply a lesson from abroad but to be ignored by the source of its inspiration, leaving it to make a lonely advance without imported technical assistance or financial aid.

Pressure from abroad is most problematic when foreign influence is concentrated on a programme that a national government regards as undesirable. Theories of external political coercion assume that money, guns, laws, or diplomatic sanctions can force the *submission* of a nominally independent state to pressures from abroad. Today's open international economy subjects every government to market pressures that can, at times, result in submission. For example, the Conservative government of John Major sought to maintain a strong British pound in foreign exchange markets. When the pound came under attack from foreign speculators in 1992, the British government more than doubled interest rates in one day in an effort to maintain its policy. However,

---

Box 7.3 External pressures and domestic responses to lessons

External pressures

	High	Low
Domestic desirability		
High	CO-OPERATE	LONELY ADVANCE
Low	SUBMISSION, NEGOTIATION, EVASION	AVOID

pressure from the foreign exchange market forced the collapse of the government's monetary policy and the devaluation of the pound to a level that stopped massive international speculation.

Military force represents the extreme form of coercive influence, but in peacetime its threatened use cannot unilaterally secure submission. At the end of the Second World War, Germany was in economic and political ruins, and authority was in the hands of occupying forces. In West Germany, the United States, Britain, and France encouraged the revival of political activity by those political and civil society groups that had been dormant or untainted by twelve years of Nazi rule. They then encouraged Germans to prepare a federal constitution in place of the unitary Weimar Republic and offered lessons drawn from their national experiences. The federal constitution could come into effect only if the occupation forces were willing to transfer their authority to a government chosen by the German people. When this occurred in 1949, it began the entrenchment of interests of elected parties, federal bureaucrats, and strong regional governments in *Länder* from Bavaria to Schleswig-Holstein with every incentive to make the new system work in the interests of their regions and citizens.

Negotiation is a common means of arriving at agreements between governments with interdependent programmes. Within the European Union, every programme is subject to multiple negotiations. Officials in the European Commission prepare initial proposals for programmes establishing standards that all member states are meant to respect to the extent that their national programme is not in harmony with these standards. Negotiations involve representatives of national governments stationed permanently at Brussels and may involve the European Parliament too, if the Parliament's approval is also necessary. The complex voting rules of the EU deprive any one national government of votes sufficient to carry a programme on its own; coalition building is required, and the disproportionate number of votes assigned to smaller countries strengthens their bargaining hand during negotiations. For those issues on which unanimity is required, then even a country as small as Luxembourg or Slovenia can threaten a veto as a means of advancing its position in negotiations.

When foreign pressures force a national government to adopt a programme that it regards as undesirable, then it can try to *evade* its commitment. The European Commission regularly reports the number of EU regulations that national governments have not yet put into effect. If a programme is particularly objectionable in national terms, then stalling tactics can be pursued indefinitely, and, if a measure is adopted, implementation and enforcement can be lax. On very important issues, evasion can be outright and flagrant. For example, for several years the French and German governments have been running national budget deficits in excess of 3.0 per cent of gross national product, which a European Central Bank programme sets as the maximum allowable deficit of euro-zone countries. In autumn 2003, the Bank confronted the French and

German governments with its record of default on its ECB obligations, a default that threatened fines of billions of euros. Both national governments rejected the Bank's pressure to adopt budget-cutting programmes as other euro-zone countries had done, and the Bank let the evasion go unpunished by any fine.

When governments of poor countries deal with institutions financed by rich countries, there is a palpable imbalance of both economic and political power, for rich countries control the purse strings and can make grants of cash conditional on recipient governments adopting programmes based on foreign ideas of what constitutes good government. The response of the recipient governments can vary from positive co-operation through sullen submission to evasion. Moreover, recipient governments retain the 'weapons of the weak' (Scott, 1985), starting with administrative control of the way that foreign-designed lessons are implemented and full control of how such programmes operate once foreign advisors have left.

The International Monetary Fund is in a strong position financially when a government approaches it for a loan because mismanagement of the economy has led to inflation spiralling out of control, goods disappearing from shops, and threats of unrest in the streets. The IMF is prepared to loan billions of dollars; it does so with conditions attached that require the borrowing government to take actions that will be politically unpopular in the short term but will stop inflation. The conditions reflect lessons from the IMF's experience in other countries that have similarly confronted runaway inflation.

A government with its national currency rapidly losing value needs the hard currency that the IMF can offer. Moreover, some officials in a country's central bank and finance ministry are likely to welcome the conditions the IMF lays down as a means of controlling the behaviour of spendthrift colleagues. The strictness of these conditions and the extent to which they are enforced depend on politics as much as economics. The more important a country is on the international scene and the stronger its allies, the less strict the conditions and the less likely they are to be enforced if the borrowing government fails to put them into effect. After reviewing the experience of the IMF in lending money to the Yeltsin government in Russia, Randall Stone (2002: xx) concludes, 'Countries that were very influential – in particular, those that received the most foreign aid from the United States – were treated very leniently and consequently were much less likely to follow IMF advice.'

Foreign aid to poor and developing countries has a different time horizon. Aid programmes of the World Bank and national counterparts are intended to promote long-term economic growth and reduce poverty, illiteracy, and malnutrition and to increase the capacity of national governments to promote these goals. In the jargon of development policy, national governments are expected to 'take ownership' of programmes, that is, to be politically committed to maintaining as its own programme whatever is kick-started by foreign aid, whether it be a new hydroelectric system or rural hospitals. In the literal sense, a national government will normally own the facilities paid for by foreign aid, and its officials will administer the programme under foreign supervision.

When an international aid institution lays down conditions for grants and loans, it faces a classic problem of agency, because it depends almost entirely on the recipient country to implement what has formally been agreed. In the implementation of a lesson, the national government has considerable discretion and international bodies are outsiders. If a foreign-funded programme is drawn from the experience of rich countries, there is unlikely to be a fit with a poor government's capacity and political priorities. Once money is in its hands, there are incentives for its officials to redefine success as using programme funds to enrich friends rather than to use it as agreed. In the worst-case scenario, corrupt officials may divert tens or hundreds of millions of dollars to local advantage while the donor agency is faced with the failure of its prescribed programme intentions.

Since foreign advisors sooner or later leave, the consequences of programmes drawn from abroad are ultimately in the hands of the national government. In the worst case, policymakers in a recipient country can concentrate on 'grants-manship', that is, getting money from abroad that can be spent to their own advantage. To do this requires designing programmes that use internationally popular buzz words, such as 'empowerment' or 'building social capital', and that *appear* to apply lessons from abroad. However, once money is in hand, actions follow local practices. For example, the British government funded a programme to provide advice to Kosovar academics about establishing a public administration programme at the University of Priština in the hope that it would train Albanian-speaking officials to administer a new regime in that semi-detached part of Serbia. The university officials accepted the money and conditions of the grant, but when the time came to appoint staff, schedules were arranged so that the key decisions about who got what jobs were made after British officials had left the country and local politics and patronage were again in command (Bache and Taylor, 2003).

Counterpressures from NGOs

The movement of ideas about how to manage an economy and about the right of citizens to civil liberties is not the exclusive preserve of national governments and intergovernmental organizations; it is also a primary concern of many non-governmental organizations (NGOs). The rise of intermestic politics has increasingly made national pressure groups turn to transnational NGOs to advance their interests. The authors of a major study of activists beyond borders declare, 'Government can no longer monopolize information flows as they could a mere half-decade ago' (Keck and Sikkink, 1998: 2).

In established democracies, national pressure groups have long existed and are accepted as part of the political process. Transnational links between pressure groups have been stimulated by: growing political interdependence, as in the European Union; institutionalized economic interdependence, as in the World Trade Organization; the increase in multinational corporations; and ease of communication through jet aeroplanes, telephones, satellite television, and the Internet. The internationalization of the media has encouraged the formation of transnational protest groups that can catch the eye of 24-hour news viewers by demonstrating in the streets at European and world summits.

Transnational networks of NGOs now advocate programmes in fields as different as the privatization of state-owned industries and women's rights. While operating as conventional pressure groups within their society, this type of NGO is distinctive because it promotes lessons drawn from other countries where their values have been put into practice. For example, privatization programmes of the Thatcher government and American affirmative action programmes have been used as models by NGOs seeking to adopt similar measures in their own country.

NGOs must operate transnationally when the problems that concern them cut across national boundaries. For example, the North American Free Trade Agreement has encouraged American trade unions to press the Mexican government to raise labour standards by applying lessons from American examples. In an interdependent free trade area, such measures are expected to benefit American workers by raising labour costs in Mexico and to make it easier for American-produced goods to compete (Teague, 2002). Organizations such as Save the Whales must lobby national governments and international fishing bodies since whales swim in and out of national jurisdictions and spend much of the year in international waters.

In new democracies and in countries that are only partly free or are unfree, NGOs are novel and may be ignored or threatened with suppression by authoritarian governors. In such circumstances, national NGOs can become transnational NGOs in the hope that they can thereby 'mobilize information strategically to help create new issues and categories and to persuade, pressure and gain leverage over much more powerful organizations and governments' (Keck and Sikkink, 1998: 2). Human rights groups need to exert pressure across national boundaries, since the national governments that are the object of their protests may literally be getting away with murder within their own country. Transnational NGOS such as Amnesty International seek the release of political prisoners and put pressure on partly free and unfree regimes to adopt laws and practices in accordance with the highest standards of free societies. Whether, and to what extent, the lessons are adopted depends on national political circumstances.

The analytic separation of organizations within a national government from transnational organizations that can exert some influence on them is useful for clarity of exposition. However, in practice the 'worlds' of national and international politics cannot be kept separate when intermestic problems arise that involve action by foreign governments and intergovernmental organizations as well as by a national government.

Vetoes are not permanent

Whereas lesson-drawing is about individuals learning what other governments are doing and creatively adapting this knowledge to design a programme for their own country, the adoption of a lesson requires commitment by the government of the day. Members of that government are telling a half-truth when they say, 'We will never do this.' What they really mean is that they will not consider it at present.

The veto an elected government can impose on a lesson is effective for the time being, but it cannot be permanent, for the authority of governors expires at the next election. Often, government is in the hands of a coalition – in many European countries a formal coalition of parties and in Washington an ad hoc coalition when government is divided with one party controlling the White House and another Congress. When this is the case, the veto on change is vulnerable to change, for coalitions are inherently unstable. Even if a lesson has been consistently ignored or rejected for decades, to project what has happened in the past into the distant future is to violate a basic political rule: never say never. For historians, the question is not whether but when political values will change.

When an election results in a change in the party and personalities controlling government, the new governors are under pressure to make things happen, introducing new programmes in place of unpopular measures that they have campaigned against. However, campaigning leaves little or no time or energy for the winners to prepare for government. The greater the level of popular dissatisfaction, the greater the incentive for a new government to turn to policy entrepreneurs offering lessons from abroad. Even if an election does not produce a change in party control of government, it can change politicians in charge of programmes in many departments. An incoming Cabinet minister usually wants to make his or her mark by doing something different. This too offers policy entrepreneurs an opening to promote lessons from abroad.

Events outside the control of government add to the contingent nature of vetoes based on values. Events can turn what was once politically unacceptable into an overriding political goal. As the English economist John Maynard Keynes once said when taxed for his apparent inconsistency, 'When the facts change, I change my mind. What do you do?' The contingency of political commitments is especially significant in economic policy, for every national economy is continuously in a state of flux, and subject to unpredictable and cyclical changes with much greater frequency than national elections. During a four-year term of office the pressure of economic events may force a government to make U-turns on taxing, spending, and/or deficits. When this occurs, governors can learn from the successes and failures of the economic programmes of other countries.

When policymakers must deal with fires in their in-trays, what was once politically impossible can rapidly become a political imperative. While many of the prophecies of doom voiced by policy entrepreneurs never come to pass, political earthquakes intermittently create fundamental upheavals in values, and politicians can no longer do what they would like to do, but do what they must do. In the American Deep South, for example, generations of white Southern politicians consistently opposed racial integration and devised increasingly ingenious programmes as obstacles to integration. Nine years after the United States Supreme Court ruled segregation unconstitutional, George Wallace declared in his inaugural address as governor of Alabama, 'Segregation now, segregation tomorrow, and segregation forever.' However, when the Federal Voting Rights Act of 1965 gave black voters a decisive voice in elections in Alabama, Governor Wallace abandoned his segregationist programmes and began canvassing for black votes. Concurrently, Britain began to witness signs of racial prejudice, as the formerly all-white country received small trickles of immigrants from the West Indies. British politicians, who had previously prided themselves on the country being free of racial prejudice, then turned to the United States to learn about anti-discrimination legislation.

Step 8
Can a lesson be applied?

A country can move forward as it is, in spite of what it is, and because of what it is.
Albert Hirschman, *Journeys toward Progress*

Even if a lesson appears desirable and the pressure of events creates a demand for action, this does not guarantee that you can apply it at home. For this to happen, there must be space to introduce a new programme into an already crowded set of government commitments; there must be the resources to implement it; and there must not be crosscultural misunderstandings that lead to a mismatch between what a lesson requires and the beliefs and practices of the government adopting it. Only if all three conditions are met can you hope to apply a lesson in practice.

Finding 'space' for a new programme in a field already crowded with existing commitments is the first requirement for applying a lesson. Given the growth of government over many generations, a newly elected government inherits hundreds of programmes from its predecessors. As the first section of this chapter shows, there are few areas of public policy where government does not already have a lot of commitments. When a new space is opened up, for example, to deal with a threatened epidemic of HIV–AIDS, there is often no readily available programme to adopt in response.

Resources are a second critical requirement, for just as you can't bake a cake without all the ingredients that are needed to make it rise, so every lesson makes claims on a multiplicity of resources involving legislation, money, personnel, and organizations. When lessons are drawn within the Anglo-American world or between OECD countries, the material and administrative resources necessary to apply a lesson can be found – if the political will is present. In developing countries, the situation is more complicated. The absence of resources is a spur to seek lessons from rich countries in the hope of substantially raising living standards, and these aspirations are often encouraged by the offer of foreign aid. However, the absence of resources often makes it difficult to implement the lessons offered and avoid wasting money or worse. As Albert Hirschman has noted, developing countries have both major assets and major liabilities. The assets can include a relatively well-educated labour force, while liabilities can include widespread corruption among public officials.

Crossnational differences are a third necessary condition of lesson-drawing, for without differences there would be nothing for one government to learn from another. The history of Japan demonstrates that great crosscultural differences can actually be an incentive to learn from other countries how to change one's own society. Differences become obstacles only when they lead to misunderstandings. Whether drawing or giving a lesson, you need to be sure that there is a fit between what policymakers want to do and what they can do. The failure to admit that good ideas are beyond a government's reach can reflect the siren call of success leading people to shut their eyes to obstacles. It can also arise from Western advisors misunderstanding how developing countries actually administer programmes.

Inheritance before choice

On entering office a new government takes an oath to uphold all the laws of the land. All the programmes that a newly elected government initially administers are a legacy from the past. This fact is often overlooked by election winners in the enthusiasm of victory. When Tony Blair became Britain's prime minister in 1997, he pledged to create a 'new' Britain, as if he could ignore an inheritance of programmes dating back centuries. However, before his first term of office was over, Blair's euphoria had disappeared and he was lashing out against his ambitions being hamstrung by the inheritance of health service programmes from half a century ago, a rail network that had evolved over more than a century, and a university system that started in the middle ages. Although American government has a much shorter history than that of Britain, and welfare legislation is newer than in Europe, an incoming US president pledged to keep taxes down nonetheless inherits spending commitments totalling well over $1 trillion a year – and a national debt that is larger still.

The collapse of one regime and its replacement by a new one would appear to offer an escape from a legacy of accumulated programmes. However, this is not the case. A new regime does not repudiate all the programmes it inherited from its predecessors, for citizens have a continuing need for education, health care, and rubbish collection, whether a regime is democratic or undemocratic. Thus, the change in political institutions between the Franco regime and a democratic regime in Spain in the 1970s transformed political institutions but not most public programmes. In Germany, which has had five different regimes in the twentieth century, welfare state programmes do not date from the fall of the Berlin Wall or the creation of the Federal Republic in 1949, but extend back to measures adopted by Bismarck in the early 1880s.

Path-dependence

The logic of path-dependence is simply stated: past commitments limit current choices – and thus what lessons can be applied. The strength of path dependence is illustrated by the fact that when Margaret Thatcher left office as Britain's prime minister after a decade of voicing commitments to cut back the size of government, more than nine-tenths of the money spent by her government went to programmes adopted by her predecessors (Rose and Davies, 1994: 120).

The adoption of programmes over the decades by policymakers dealing with different pressures creates a set of programmes that are 'sticky', that is, hard to modify, because it creates interests with the expectation that policy will continue down the same path in future. Path-dependence 'locks in' the government of the day by limiting its scope for choice. Since today's programmes reflect past commitments, this implies that the government of the day can endorse programmes that add to what is done. However, any choice must take into account what has gone before (North, 1990: 93ff.; Neustadt and May, 1986: 105ff.; Pierson, 2000). As long as established commitments generate satisfaction, policymakers have limited incentive to learn from abroad.

Whereas best-practice recommendations offer lessons for the future, path-dependence is a reminder of the importance of past commitments. Pension programmes accumulated over a century can throw a shadow more than half a century into the future (Box 8.1). In Britain the first old age pension law was enacted in 1908 for a restricted number of workers who managed to live well beyond their normal life expectancy. Since then, the number of people benefiting has been increased by the lowering of the age for receiving a pension and by improvements in health increasing the number of people living longer in old age. In addition, criteria of eligibility have been altered so that everyone who has been employed can draw a pension. The cost has also risen as the sum paid has been adjusted to take into account inflation and economic growth. While all the initial beneficiaries of the 1908 Act are now dead, some people drawing pensions today started work before the Second World War. The median employee paying social security taxes was born in 1965 and will not expect to draw a full pension until the year 2030. The youngest group of workers paying social security contributions will expect to draw a full pension until the year 2070 or beyond. The pension of today's youthful workers will be financed in part by taxes paid by people who will be drawing their pension in the second quarter of the twenty-second century.

Path-dependent programmes are obstacles to new measures. While any newly elected government could, in theory, repeal existing pension programmes in favour of a free market programme based on the model of Chile, it would take generations before the full impact of doing so was evident. To avoid destitution among the elderly and meet obligations to today's contributors, repeal legislation would have to continue paying pensions authorized by inherited legislation for as long as half a century into the future.

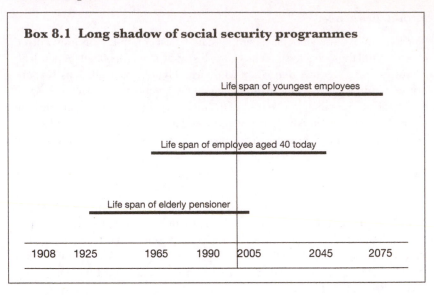

Box 8.1 Long shadow of social security programmes

Life span of youngest employees

Life span of employee aged 40 today

Life span of elderly pensioner

| 1908 | 1925 | 1965 | 1990 | 2005 | 2045 | 2075 |

When a path-dependent programme confers benefits on a group, this creates strong pressures against adopting lessons from abroad that threaten their interests. For example, for two decades the German economy has been causing dissatisfaction to governors and governed as the economy has grown very slowly, unemployment has risen above 10 per cent to the highest level in more than half a century, and the public deficit has risen too. Concurrently, German policymakers have diagnosed restrictive 'social market' legislation inherited from the past as a major obstacle to economic recovery. Many European Union countries as well as the United States offer lessons about ways to deregulate an economy in order to promote economic growth. However, political interests and values have led German governments of both right and left to hesitate to adopt such programmes.

Path-dependent programmes have a tendency to become inefficient with the passage of time. Unlike best-practice programmes, they are not state-of-the-art measures. Instead, path-dependent programmes are an amalgam of measures patched together over time by many different hands in many different circumstances (David, 1985). For example, the *acquis communautaire* of the European Union does not represent the best practices of national governments. It is the accumulation of programmes that member states have agreed in the past. The EU programme that claims the most money, the common agricultural policy, was introduced in 1958 as a means of providing income support to peasants on small plots of land, who were politically important because of their numbers. While most of the peasants have disappeared, the common agricultural policy continues on its established path.

At a given moment in time, nothing appears to have a tighter grip on policymakers than the dead hand of the past. Yet this is a short-term view. While a programme may remain constant, changes do occur in the policy environment in which it originated. When this happens, the resulting misfit between an established programme and its environment will cause its effectiveness to deteriorate. This in turn will begin to generate dissatisfaction. Policymakers can respond by making modifications and amendments to a programme. The longer signals of dissatisfaction are ignored, the greater the pressure for change will be, encouraging innovation and the search for lessons from abroad.

The wicked context problem

Most fields of public policy are 'brown field' sites built up over the years by successive governments each adding a programme or two. The result is a crowded space with limited ground for erecting new programmes and requires any new measure to take into account neighbouring programmes, or even to clear ground by repealing an old programme in order to find space for a new one. This creates a 'wicked context' problem for proponents of introducing a lesson based on a foreign example, for its innovative value will depend on its being different from what went before, yet its success will depend on how well it integrates with other programmes to which it must relate in the same field.

Inserting a lesson into a crowded policy field produces friction, because the new programme will compete with established programmes for public attention, political support, and cash. However small the apparent cost of a new programme, it must come out of a department's existing budget, reducing spending on established programmes, or else compete with established programmes for any extra public funding available. For these reasons, there is a risk that even if a lesson is adopted it may be underfunded.

Even if widespread dissatisfaction with an established programme creates a demand for a new measure, the more central the cause of dissatisfaction the more difficult it is to introduce a root-and-branch change because of the spillover effects of change on other programmes. Hence, for social security or health insurance programmes established half a century or a century ago, it is much easier to amend an existing programme than to introduce a new measure. If a lesson is to have a chance of being applied, it should be limited in scope. Given the scale of health and social security policies, even a measure that is limited in scope can have an impact on the lives of millions of people.

Failure can also result if a lesson is introduced without supporting measures. For example, British government attempts to promote American-style private finance for higher education ignore contextual characteristics that generate billions of dollars in endowments in the United States. British universities lack the endowments that private US universities have accumulated over more than a century. They also lack the large number of graduates that are accustomed to making annual gifts to their alma mater as individuals, and the alumni in state legislatures that promote interests of state universities there. Moreover, British universities do not have the religious affiliations that provide a constituency of support for many private American colleges. While British parents are prepared to spend large sums on secondary schooling, they do not expect to pay for university tuition, whereas in the United States the opposite tends to be the case. In such circumstances, to import American fund-raising methods in a context lacking these associated features would lead to financial disappointment.

When a novel problem arises, such as genetically modified food, policymakers will face an 'empty sky' problem because of the absence of potentially relevant programmes. While this lack of prior history imposes few inherited constraints on government choice, unfamiliarity means there are no rules of thumb for diagnosing what is happening. When the problem is common to many national governments, as is the case with genetically modified food, the opportunities for learning from abroad are increased. If one or two countries take the initiative, they can be trend-setters and get the credit by running the risk of going first. If many countries respond at the same time with different measures, then this offers the opportunity to benchmark one's own national achievement and learn from the successes and failures of other countries.

Resource limitations

Before applying a lesson, policymakers must verify that they have the resources needed to make it work. Just as societies differ in their resources, so programmes differ in the claims that they make on laws, money, human capital, and organizations. Programmes about marriage and divorce are law-intensive; pension programmes can be administered with relatively few public employees but require a great deal of money; and health and education programmes are both labour- and money-intensive. Hence, the extent to which resource limits affect the adoption of a lesson depends on the problem. While a poor country will lack the money needed to adopt a Scandinavian pension system, it can reduce population growth by drawing lessons from Scandinavian laws promoting birth control and abortion. One thing is constant: no programme is cost-free in its claims on resources.

Applying a lesson across national boundaries requires translating *laws* from one legal system to another. Studies of comparative legal systems usually emphasize differences in legal philosophy between Roman law systems of Europe and the English common law tradition found in the Anglo-American world. In practice, differences between legal systems are usually not a significant obstacle to applying a lesson. For example, a social security programme can be enacted in a Roman law or in a common law system; the substance of the programme remains the same. When programmes are interdependent, as is invariably the case with laws affecting international trade, there is great pressure for harmonizing procedural differences.

Differences between legal systems may affect the way in which a programme is enforced. Whereas American data protection acts rely more on individuals to protect their rights through the courts, similar European programmes place greater responsibility for enforcing data protection on public agencies. More difficult problems arise when key terms in a programme do not have the same meaning in different national settings. For example, unemployment programmes assume a worker either is or is not in paid employment. However, in developing countries a person may juggle two jobs, one in the official economy and one in the shadow economy, and in rural economies women may be full-time unpaid family workers.

Money is a greater resource limitation than laws. However, the cost of the average government programme is relatively low. Because public expenditure is divided among hundreds of discrete measures, even when a field such as health counts for a large sum, it does so because of the total cost of dozens of different programmes from ante-natal care for pregnant women to specialist treatment of geriatric patients, and much in between. The median public programme costs much less than 1 per cent of public expenditure, and a new programme usually costs even less because it has not yet had time to grow to its full size. The cost of applying a lesson is often less than the margin of error that government makes when forecasting its annual tax revenue.

When governors of prosperous countries say they cannot find the money to adopt a lesson, this usually means that other programmes have priority. Thus, the governments of rich Scandinavian countries do not fund programmes to train astronauts, while the American federal government does not finance programmes to provide paternity leave for working males when their partner has a baby. There are big differences too in the amount of taxes that governments are prepared to levy in order to finance public expenditure. Whereas government spending in Sweden is equal to 55 per cent of its gross domestic product, in Japan it accounts for only 30 per cent of GDP.

Even relatively poor countries can find some money to finance programmes to which they give a high priority. Ethiopia is among the poorest countries in the world; its national income is estimated at less than $100 per person. Yet Ethiopia nonetheless spends 8 per cent of its national income on defence. By international standards, the per capita gross domestic product of both India and Pakistan is very low, but each national government can find the money to finance nuclear weapons. From Bangladesh to Nigeria and Haiti, much money that ought to be spent on development programmes is siphoned into the pockets of corrupt officials.

When costly programmes are involved, such as providing free health care or pensions for all citizens, money is an obstacle to poor countries importing lessons from rich countries. At the time of the creation of the People's Republic of China half a century ago, the country was very poor. Initially, the Communist government of Mao Tse-Tung sought to substitute ideology for money, and looked to the Soviet Union and Marxist-Leninist principles for lessons. Today China seeks economic growth from the market; a side effect of this has been a crisis in social welfare. To find programmes that could be implemented with Chinese resources, the government could turn to newly industrializing Asian countries, where welfare planning is 'productivist', as spending on welfare is contingent on the economy first producing the resources needed to finance these programmes (Holliday, 2000; Rose, 2003b: 14ff.). Alternatively, it could examine Japan, where the household has produced a great deal of welfare without state finance (cf. Rose, 1986). However, the attractive power of rich, successful countries encourages many Chinese experts to study social welfare programmes that they cannot afford to adopt (Box 8.2).

Qualified personnel are required to deliver many types of public programmes. In small countries, the population of the country prevents government from adopting military programmes that require large numbers of people. The biggest European member of NATO, Germany, has less than one-third the population of the United States and the median NATO member state has a population of only 4 per cent of the United States. Hence, most NATO members cannot adopt military programmes modelled on what is done in that country. Population size

---

Box 8.2 What can Chinese learn from Europe about welfare?

The Chinese Communist government is promoting economic growth by introducing market forces in place of the central controls of a command economy. This requires state-owned enterprises to increase productivity by reducing the number of employees that they have, or go bankrupt. Since employees of state-owned enterprises usually rely on the enterprise for welfare benefits such as health care, housing, and pensions, this is creating a crisis in the Chinese system of welfare affecting tens of millions of employees.

The Chinese Academy of the Social Sciences in Beijing is sending senior scholars to examine welfare state programmes abroad as a substitute for openly debating this fundamental and troubling policy issue within China. Public agencies in the West have been forthcoming with money to enable Chinese social scientists to visit Europe to learn about programmes providing social welfare there.

European welfare specialists tell Chinese visitors that countries such as Sweden and Britain today face a 'crisis' of the welfare state. However, the European definition of crisis is the opposite of that in China. The European crisis arises from the fact that spending on health, education, and social security claims so much (critics say 'too much') money. By contrast, in China, where per capita cash income is less than 5 per cent of that of Northern Europe, China's welfare crisis arises from the fact that inefficient state-owned firms no longer have enough money to meet all the costs of welfare measures.

Source: Finer, 2003, and personal experience of the author.

also affects the suitability of employment programmes. When unemployment rises in countries such as Ireland and Denmark, policymakers look for lessons that will promote thousands of jobs, whereas when unemployment rises in countries such as Germany or France, policymakers need programmes that will create hundreds of thousands of jobs.

A shortage of public personnel is a greater constraint on lesson-drawing in developing countries, for providing higher education or sophisticated surgery requires high levels of skill. Yet many jobs in the public sector are low-level clerical jobs or manual tasks, such as maintaining office files or mending roads. In developing countries, the majority of the population usually has the skills required for routine jobs and the scarcity of alternative sources of employment makes a civil service job attractive. Where education limits the pool of highly skilled labour, people can be trained abroad if the numbers required are not large. However poor their country, most governments can find the people who can be trained to fly military aircraft and operate a national airline.

Without *organization*, laws, money, and personnel cannot be combined to apply a lesson. Contemporary specialists in new public management debate the merits of different ways of organizing the delivery of public services. The conclusion is that there is no one best way to organize a government and that many different organizational forms are consistent with a given programme goal. For example, a government-funded health service may provide hospital care through municipal hospitals, state-owned facilities, not-for-profit bodies and religious foundations, or profit-making hospitals – or by a combination of all of these.

Before a lesson can be applied it must be approved – and the political clout of established organizations is a major influence on whether or not a lesson is adopted. Public organizations are inclined to define the 'public interest' in terms matching their own organizational interest. As political insiders, heads of government organizations are well placed to demand concessions as the price of supporting a programme. The more decentralized the system of decision making (for example, Washington as against Whitehall), the more a lesson is likely to be amended as the price of securing adoption.

If a new programme is approved, in OECD countries the organizational resources are usually available. Office space, computer networks, and back office staff are available to administer the new programme; rules and regulations can be based on the government's established practices; and civil servants can be re-assigned or borrowed from other programmes and agencies.

The attempt to apply lessons from the developed world to developing countries shows that it is not the form but the effectiveness of public sector organizations that is critical. In a modern system of administration, drawing lessons from the computer experience of another government involves marginal learning, for computer networking is familiar in both places. However, many developing countries lack the organizational technology necessary to benefit

Box 8.3 Leaping to apply computers without looking

In modern states, bureaucratic procedures were introduced into government a century ago and computers a generation ago. Hence, the preconditions for computer use were present even before computers became standard items of office equipment. Given the pressures to modernize public administration in developing countries, international advisors sometimes recommend information technology as a means of leapfrogging over intermediate stages in organizational reform and immediately creating state-of-the-art public administration.

On the advice of a Western management consultancy firm and with money from Western aid agencies, the government of Ghana introduced a computerized integrated personnel and payroll database system. Success of the programme required entering into the computer system accurate data from existing paper files of the government. However, the government's files had many names of 'ghost' workers, that is, people it no longer employed. When existing public employees were asked to provide fresh information about themselves for entry to the new system, some gave incorrect information in order to increase their pay and promotion prospects and some did not return forms. Thus, the computerized database of public personnel gave a false picture of the people the government was actually employing. Other shortcomings of the new system meant that in a single month as many as 15,000 education employees went unpaid.

Source: Cain, 1999.

from connecting to the Internet. While this does not stop Western advisors from offering the 'best and the brightest' lessons to poor countries, it does frustrate success (Box 8.3).

For a lesson to be effective, it must also be administered honestly. When goods and services are diverted from those entitled to receive them to those who want to pocket benefits to which they are not entitled, both effectiveness and integrity are lost. Moreover, awarding contracts to incompetent suppliers or allowing contractors to get by with erecting shoddy hospital buildings or roads will lead to new facilities going out of service or operating at half-speed because they so often need repairs. If teachers extort cash payments for 'free' schoolbooks from parents and children, or fail to turn up at school because they can make more money that day at another job, poorer children will get little or no education.

Mutual misunderstandings

Lesson-drawing is a two-way process, involving an exchange of knowledge between two countries and programme experts who may or may not share a common set of cultural beliefs. Within the European Union, constant interaction between policymakers facing similar problems provides some understanding of how other governments see common problems. Within international epistemic communities, professionals from different continents can have a common understanding of professional concerns – but that is not the same as understanding the political and cultural context in which each must operate. The recurrent problems of fitting programmes justified by universalistic economic theories to developing nations is a reminder that, while shared beliefs and programme knowledge are necessary, they are not sufficient to ensure that a lesson can be applied. The old saying, 'The devil is in the details', is particularly relevant in policymaking.

Because lesson-drawing is about moving programmes across national boundaries, the potential for misunderstandings is greater than within a national political system. While crossnational cultural differences are numerous, their potential for conflict can easily be exaggerated. To an anthropologist, the meal habits or dress codes of civil servants appear to be of cultural importance, but to a policy analyst differences in food and clothing are of consequence only if they have a demonstrable effect on how programmes work.

Cultural beliefs

Cultural beliefs and norms about how the world works can create major obstacles to applying lessons. One difficulty that Western advisors have in dealing with AIDS epidemics in parts of Africa is that local practices that international public health experts see as causes of an AIDS epidemic, such as promiscuous and unprotected sex, are regarded as normal practices in some African societies. The president of South Africa has even rejected medical evidence of the causes of AIDS in favour of a political diagnosis of the disease.

Lessons rest on beliefs about how the world works, including how citizens will respond to a lesson imported from another country. Economists are often explicit in linking specific programme advice to assumptions that are the basis of the neo-classical economic theories of how markets work. The linkage of theory and practice was also a central claim of Marxist economics, but it made production rather than profit its central focus. The collapse of the Soviet system did not change overnight Russian beliefs about how an economy works. Opinion surveys since found that many Russians continue to believe that you do not get what you pay for, but that you get what you can through connections; businessmen who make money are not helping to make the economy grow but are intelligent, hardworking, political manipulators and dishonest; and that big state factories should not lay off workers but continue producing goods even if no one wants to buy their output (Rose, 2002).

Confronted with the economic void in post-Communist economies, Western economic advisors were ready to prescribe lessons based on their theories about how the world worked. For example, economist Richard Portes told an

International Monetary Fund seminar that post-Communist countries did not need to build a new economy from scratch. Instead, he recommended that all they had to do was 'simply copy applicable legislation from the European Community' (quoted in Khanna, 1991: 278). However, Portes's belief in the effectiveness of economic legislation was not matched by Russian entrepreneurs, who believed that they could get rich quick by acting on the old Russian proverb, 'The law is like a door in the middle of the field. You can go through it if you want, but you don't have to.' In the struggle for the control of valuable state enterprises, Russian beliefs took precedence over Western-inspired legislation.

When advisors and recipients of advice have very different agendas, the politics of giving and receiving advice encourages misunderstandings. Foreign advisors often have an agenda of recommendations that they carry from country to country. For example, because of their organizational goals and professional training, International Monetary Fund staff give priority to programmes that will reduce inflation and government deficits. Whereas IMF economists are in the business of saving currencies, national policymakers receiving their advice usually give priority to saving their control of government and view IMF recommendations as threatening to destroy their hold on power.

The conditions in which Western advisors are employed to give programme advice and money create incentives for advisors to think in terms of how their advice fits with the political beliefs and guidelines laid down by their superiors in Washington, in a UN agency in New York, or in Europe, as well as how it fits with local conditions. There is no guarantee that the conditions for funding advice laid down by donor agencies will suit the conditions of developing countries targeted for assistance. When policymakers in developing countries realize this, the lesson that they may draw is that foreign aid is not so much about promoting development as it is about grantsmanship, that is, getting money for programmes that foreign governments will pay for.

The greater the cultural differences between countries, the greater the need for foreign advisors to listen to those to whom they tender advice. The principles set out for policymakers in Box 8.4 – approach a country with an open mind, ask questions of responsible officials, assess available programme resources, and be flexible – may appear to be no more than common courtesy and common sense. Yet both can be lacking when foreign advisors meet officials of an alien government whose programmes are in a mess. When prompt action is required, there is a temptation for advisors to take the short cut of telling troubled officials what they ought to do. If this is done before advisors learn what a government can do, then failure is the likely result.

Desirability, practicality, or both?

Deciding whether or not to adopt a lesson involves both political evaluation of the goal of a programme and expert assessment of its means. Politicians give

---

Box 8.4 What advisors who give lessons need to learn

1 Approach an unfamiliar country with a mind that is free of preconceptions about how similar or different it is from your own country.

2 Ask questions of responsible officials there about why existing programmes operate as they do, what problems they are meant to deal with, and what problems they create for the government.

3 Inventory the resources available for current programmes in your field and estimate the money, personnel, and political capital available to support new measures.

4 Ransack your mind for examples from other countries of programmes that appear to fit the situation at hand.

5 Brainstorm with people in the country about changes that *might* be introduced. If people resist the idea of change, emphasize the costs of doing nothing. If people endorse a lesson you offer, press them to explain how they would deal with obstacles to introducing it.

6 Accept a programme only loosely inspired by lessons you can offer – as long as it is likely to improve conditions within a country and there is a good chance that national policymakers will implement it.

---

priority to value judgements, while experts are professionally inclined to concentrate on its means.

A judgement about ends is a value judgement – are the programme's goals desirable or, at the least, acceptable? – and there are value conflicts both within and between countries. To assume that lesson-drawing is simply a matter of determining whether a programme can be applied without considering whether it should be adopted is to take the politics out of policymaking.

To concentrate on the desirability of a programme without considering whether it is feasible in a given national context is to turn policymaking into a process of wish-fulfilment. You should also evaluate a proposed programme to see whether it can be introduced within an existing field of policy without being crippled; whether there are sufficient resources to implement it; and whether the assumptions underlying the programme are understood and accepted by the government receiving a lesson as well as by foreign advisors.

Logically, the desirability and practicality of lessons can be combined in four different ways (Box 8.5). Two combinations are easy to handle. If a proposed programme is evaluated as desirable and its resource claims are within the reach of a national government, then it is doubly attractive to both politicians and technical experts. If both groups evaluate a programme is undesirable and required resources are not available, it is irrelevant and can readily be rejected.

If technical experts say a programme is practical but politicians see it as undesirable, then it is an unwanted technical solution. If the measure is of low

---

Box 8.5 Two standards for evaluating a lesson

Programme desirability

	High	Low
Practicality		
High	DOUBLY ATTRACTIVE	UNWANTED SOLUTION
Low	SIREN CALL	IRRELEVANT

---

visibility, for example, a reform of procedures within a government agency, and resource costs are low, then experts may quietly push ahead with a change that will make their work easier. However, the only lessons that can be adopted by stealth are those of little or no political significance.

If a foreign programme appears attractive, politicians will want action. However, the demand for a lesson does not guarantee that the resources are available. When a lesson is politically attractive but resources are lacking, it is a siren call. Foreign advisors who unthinkingly prescribe attractive programmes beyond the capacity of a country to implement them are like the sirens in Homer's *Ulysses*, encouraging governors to steer the ship of state in the direction of what is appealing and ignore warnings from their expert crew that adopting a programme impossible to attain threatens a shipwreck on the rocks.

Step 9

Increasing chances of success

Conserve energy. Don't try harder; try better.
Office poster

Since the record of every government is a combination of successes and failures, lesson-drawing has two faces: it is about learning ways to make programmes better *and* about learning how to avoid measures resulting in failure. A simplistic approach to policy transfer ignores the distinction between positive and negative learning; prudent policymakers do not. Understanding the reasons why a programme has been tried and has failed elsewhere is a form of preventive policymaking: it can inoculate a government against making an avoidable mistake.

Because policymakers are activists, drawing positive lessons is a bigger priority than learning what not to do. That is why this chapter focuses on increasing chances of success. The fact that a lesson is based on a programme in operation elsewhere demonstrates that it can be successful – all other conditions remaining equal. The *ceteris paribus* qualification familiar from economics textbooks should be treated as a warning light, for even though a programme works in another country, this is no guarantee that it can be applied at home. It signifies the need to verify whether all other conditions are equal. If this is not the case, then a lesson must be adapted in order to increase its chances of success.

The old adage – 'Never say never in politics' – applies to lesson-drawing too. It is just as arrogant to assert that a lesson can never work as to assert that it will succeed when failure appears more likely. The critical questions are under what circumstances and to what extent a lesson can be successfully applied. From an instrumentalist perspective, the task is not only to identify obstacles to introducing a programme but also to find ways of overcoming such obstacles.

Making the most of contingencies

Because policymaking is an uncertain activity, the likelihood of a lesson being successfully applied is contingent. The crucial analytic question is: under what circumstances and to what extent could a programme in operation elsewhere work here? Inevitably, the answer will reflect both general differences between two national contexts and the nuts-and-bolts details of a specific programme. While policymakers can do little about structural differences, they do control the design of the lesson based on foreign experience. While control does not extend as far as providing unlimited amounts of money to underwrite a new programme, there are lots of things they can do when designing a programme to make it more effective (Box 9.1). *The likelihood of a lesson being applied successfully is greater if:*

1   *There is a clearly defined objective.* Vagueness has its uses in political rhetoric. When campaigning for office, Tony Blair responded to challenges about his programme by promising to do 'what works'. The answer was part of his strategy to attract the broadest possible electoral support, since there is no chance that anyone would vote for a prime minister who promised to do 'what doesn't work'. However, a pledge to do what works can mean anything or nothing. It leaves officials asked to design a programme that works clueless about what the prime minister wants done or in what direction to search for ideas. And in many fields of public policy, halfway through his second term of office, Blair was still searching for programmes that work.

    A clear definition of the problem is the starting point of drawing a successful lesson. A vague injunction to 'do something' about crime can lead government departments to relabel as crime prevention measures programmes dealing with everything from preschool education to credit card regulations. If, however, the problem is defined as stopping credit card crime this makes clear what the objective is – and it implies a different kind of programme than what would be designed to reduce the number of juvenile criminals.

Box 9.1 Conditions increasing success in applying lessons

1   There is a clearly defined objective.
2   There is a single goal.
3   The programme has a simple design.
4   It is based on tested social, political, and technical knowledge.
5   There is flexibility in relating the elements of a programme.
6   Political leaders are committed.

---

2   *There is a single goal.* Any programme must have limits to its scope and each government department has limits to its responsibilities. Designing a programme is like playing tennis; the secret of success is to keep your eye on the ball in front of you and to resist the temptation to turn a programme into a solution for all of a government's problems. While the management of the economy involves multiple goals, there are many government departments concerned with different aspects of economic affairs, such as fighting inflation, reducing unemployment, raising tax revenue, promoting foreign trade, encouraging new firms, and controlling public expenditure. If a government department fails to do what it is particularly charged to do, it risks being abolished as useless. If it tries to encroach on the responsibilities of other departments, it invites a turf war that can consume all its political capital.

   If a programme does not have a single primary goal, then these multiple intentions can lead to it being evaluated as good in parts and bad in parts. Economists can take multiple consequences into account, assigning each a value as a cost or benefit in order to arrive at a net cost/benefit ratio. However, identifying multiple consequences will make visible a number of potential costs and thus feed opposition that can prevent a programme being adopted. Politicians want support for the primary objective of a programme, and are prepared to externalize (that is, ignore) unintended and unpopular side effects. As Lindblom (1965: 145–146) has explained, 'Forthright neglect of important consequences is a noteworthy problem-solving tactic.' In pursuit of their own ends, politicians can leave to other government agencies, to the private sector, or to individuals the task of minimizing unwanted side effects.

3   *The programme has a simple design.* Policymakers like simplicity, for the simpler a programme is, the easier it is to relate a proposal to a desired goal. Policy analysts appreciate simplicity too, because fewer assumptions need to be made about the cause-and-effect relationships required to make a programme succeed.

   The simplest programme has a direct link between a single cause and a single effect. Such simplicity can be achieved if the goal is to repeal an existing programme, for example, to repeal laws that make cannabis illegal. Before doing so, policymakers can look at foreign examples to see what the consequences have been of repeal and also to look at efforts to enforce anti-cannabis laws more effectively. However, repeal measures can easily become complicated and have unintended second-order consequences, as the privatization of state-owned enterprises demonstrates. While the principle of ridding the state of ownership of many industries was clear, policymakers were confronted with a multiplicity of choices about the way in which a particular industry could be sold off, and the options differed between countries and even between industries within a country. In addition, policymakers learned that disposing of ownership did not dispose of all responsibility for regulating major utilities in the public interest. This too brought about a choice between alternative programmes for regulating prices, safety, and standards of service. Before making a choice, policymakers could draw lessons about what could be done and what should be avoided from their previous privatization measures and from foreign examples.

To have a chance of achieving a goal, all the necessary elements for success must be included in the design of a programme. Success depends on distinguishing between necessary elements and superfluous details. While many details are necessary, it is a mistake to think that everything, from the logo emblem of a new agency to its office hours, is as important as its budget and conditions for spending money. The opposite of a vague and dismissive attitude towards the nuts and bolts of a programme is trying to micro-manage activities. For example, while president of the United States, Jimmy Carter went so far as to get involved in details of the allocation of time on the White House tennis courts. Many British prime ministers have veered between distancing themselves from the day-to-day activities of government departments and, when a crisis blows up, attempting to micro-manage in a field to which they have given little or no attention previously.

There is a danger of being 'too simple by half', reducing knowledge to a few general principles. For example, President of the World Bank James D. Wolfensohn describes 'four lessons on building effective institutions distilled from Bank experience. They are to: identify institutions that work and those that do not; complement existing resources; promote links between economic actors; and promote competition' (World Bank, 2002a: iii–iv). Such general propositions certainly avoid getting bogged down in detail, but they fail to identify the programmatic means to put these principles into practice.

4   *It relies on tested social and technical knowledge.* Programmes require both social *and* technical skills. The knowledge needed to conduct surgery, teach mathematics, or fight fires is technical, while organizing these skills in hospitals, schools, and fire departments is social. Government has grown because of the development of bodies of knowledge that enable policymakers to build more hospitals, schools, and fire departments in the confident expectation that they will meet their programme objectives (see Rose, 1988).

Most programmes of modern government draw on a substantial amount of social and technical knowledge. In every country with compulsory education, children are expected to learn to read soon after starting school. Although reading is taught in more than fifty different languages, there are not fifty different ways to teach reading; the core of common practice is greater still in teaching arithmetic. In such circumstances, it is an extreme form of nationalism to claim that a government concerned about the low educational achievement of pupils can learn nothing by looking at other countries. When a lesson is vetoed as politically unacceptable, this is often a tacit admission that, even though the programme could be applied here, we do not want to introduce it.

The knowledge base of an innovatory programme cannot be tested to the same extent as that of long-established programmes, for even if the logic of an innovation is impeccable it is unsupported by experience. The first country that adopts an innovatory programme is at risk of learning the hard way about its shortcomings. The risk is reduced for the second, third, and subsequent countries adopting a programme. By the time half a dozen different countries have adopted an innovation, it is no longer novel and there is a substantial amount of knowledge about how it works. This improves the chances for success of countries that follow on after the innovators, for they are drawing lessons from programmes that have been 'de-bugged' by innovators. While there remain crossnational obstacles in applying a lesson, they are usually less than the innovator's risk of going first.

5   *There is flexibility in relating the elements of a programme.* Non-applicable lessons are easy to create: all that is required is a photocopier and insensitivity to context. The photocopier makes it possible to photocopy laws, organization charts, and budgets of a programme already in operation elsewhere. An advisor insensitive to context can recommend the programme for application in other countries, whether there is a match or a mismatch in values and resources. But even when backed up by financial assistance or sanctions, a lesson prescribed by an advisor anxious to spread a programme will fail if it is a photocopy that has not been adapted to fit a different context. After making a portable model of how a programme works in a foreign country, the policymakers responsible must make three types of alterations before it can be successfully applied (Box 9.2). There is a need to subtract elements that constitute obstacles to adoption; to add fresh elements to make a proposal politically and operationally viable; and to link together all the elements so that the new lesson will not be amended to death, but instead produce the satisfaction that initially made a foreign example attractive.

The first thing to do when creating a lesson is to subtract references to foreign institutions and laws. A model should be abstracted from national experience, for only generic elements can be transported across national boundaries. Furthermore, if there are non-essential elements of a programme that would invite controversy in an importing country – for example, a preamble stating that its goal is to redistribute income – they can be deleted to avoid alienating potential allies without any other effect. However, deleting an element that is essential can destabilize a computerized

---

Box 9.2 Ways of introducing flexibility when lesson-drawing

SUBTRACTION

Eliminate irrelevant references to foreign institutions and laws.

Discard elements that invite controversy, such as a preamble that invokes non-consensual values.

Remove references to resource requirements that are absent in the adopting country, such as a national identity card.

ADDITION

Introduce functionally equivalent elements, such as a driver's license or social security number to compensate for the removal of references to a national identity card.

Add national features that make a programme more effective or politically more attractive.

Accept political demands for additions, as long as the cost of doing so is marginal rather than destructive of the programme's purpose.

Invent novel elements when confronted with a challenge for which standard operating procedures offer no solution.

LINKAGE

For every element removed from a programme, make sure a compensating change is made to avoid the loss of effectiveness.

Make sure that every element added to a programme has a net positive effect or is simply 'window-dressing' without a negative impact.

---

flow chart. A policy analyst should consider the flashing warning on a VDU a positive benefit; they are an electronic reminder that removing one essential of a programme will have an impact on other parts.

The subtraction of a necessary element of a programme requires the *addition* of a new element to substitute for what has been taken out. Otherwise, the amended programme will fail. For example, if a programme involves charging users to determine access and raise revenue, and a social democratic government is against charges, then it must introduce an alternative means of allocating the service, for example, having people queue indefinitely or increasing taxation.

Distinctive national conditions, for example, a dispersed rural population or a minority language group, may require the addition of features to address needs not faced by the exporting country. In principle, substituting elements does not threaten success, for any systematic review of programmes dealing with a common problem of modern countries will show that there are a variety of ways to achieve a given objective. A greater risk of jeopardizing success arises when national politics requires the addition of elements to satisfy groups with the potential power to veto a new programme.

If there is neither time nor resources to search the world, policymakers can invent elements to fill the gaps in a programme that is otherwise complete. In doing this, policymakers are not speculating in a void. Instead, their scope for invention is focused on specific gaps in a programme. Whatever new element is considered must be convincingly justified in terms of fitting interlocking parts of the programme.

Linking the parts of a new programme together is like completing a puzzle. The starting point is the model that constitutes the source of the lesson (see Box 5.1). The removal of unnecessary or unwanted parts of the model creates gaps that must be filled by adding elements that are functionally equivalent. If the preliminary result is that a few parts do not quite fit together and a few appear surplus, policymakers must show their artfulness by making modifications that will produce a programme design that is focused on the object at hand.

The process of adding and subtracting parts to a model makes it a new programme not only in its national context but also because it differs from the foreign example that was its prototype. When a lesson is an adaptation of a programme from a single country, many of its parts can readily be traced to its origin. When a lesson is a hybrid synthesizing parts from programmes in several countries, the lesson can appear as a novelty even though its constituent parts can be traced back to their different sources.

6 *Political leaders are committed.* The most carefully designed lesson will be put into effect only if there is political commitment from governors. If a lesson is primarily technical, the formal endorsement of elected officeholders is needed to provide legitimacy. When a lesson is based on a programme that is well established elsewhere, the controversy that greeted it initially is often forgotten. However, introducing a similar programme in a different national context will stir up controversy if it is politically important. Taking a decision in the midst of controversy not only requires the capacity to evaluate criticisms of a programme; it also requires the political guts to confront and, if necessary, overrule critics.

In the era of colonialism, imperial authorities could impose programmes on their colonies; this process continued up to the achievement of independence. Many imposed programmes and institutions, such as a British-style system of parliamentary government, soon collapsed due to a lack of political commitment from new rulers who preferred what they described as indigenous forms and that their critics described as dictatorship.

Manipulating foreign symbols

Once politicians are committed to a lesson, politics takes over from policy analysis. To put a lesson into effect requires shifting from policy design to the politics of marketing. In every marketplace of ideas, there are advocates of new programmes showing their wares and defenders of the status quo protecting their interests. To market a lesson, proponents must tell a story that is appealing and compelling. Whereas policy analysis is about the careful linkage of cause and effect, political marketing is about mobilizing support for or against a programme.

Stories can achieve political effect by invoking symbols in witty one-line phrases. The protean character of symbols makes them useful weapons in political controversy, for they can be adapted to suit political tastes. When the object is to market rather than design a programme, vague symbols are an asset, for the great majority of the public is uninterested in the details of programmes. The symbols associated with a programme are meant to stack the cards in its favour in political debate, for example, describing a bill as about Homeland Security or the Prevention of Terrorism.

Policymakers have always invoked symbols of their national past 'for advocacy or for comfort' (Neustadt and May, 1986: xii). American policymakers are invariably ready to invoke 'the American way' as the best way to do things and politicians can ignore lessons from abroad or treat them as alien to the American way. In the days of the Soviet Union, its governors proudly promoted programmes associated with Marxist-Leninist principles and rejected lessons from abroad as reflecting alien forms of capitalist exploitation. In Russia today, President Putin veers between proudly invoking Russia's traditions, without specifying what this means for contemporary public policy, and seeking ways to enable the Russian economy to escape from its Soviet legacy. British politicians have intermittently gone through bouts of national pride, proclaiming that whatever is British is best, and periods of self-doubt that stress the need to adopt new programmes to keep up or catch up with foreigners. While proud of national traditions, policymakers in small countries often accept that bigger countries know things that they do not and are less inclined to be distracted by nationalist symbols.

When there is dissatisfaction with a national programme, politicians can no longer invoke symbols of national tradition. A lesson from abroad supplies foreign symbols that can readily be used for ammunition in debate. In an effort to discredit a proposal, opponents will attempt to create guilt by association, linking it with many things from its country of origin, ranging from unfamiliar foods or a sluggish economy to failure in football competitions. For example, when President Eisenhower was asked what he thought of a social democratic programme in Sweden, he dismissed it out of hand on the grounds that he didn't want Americans to commit suicide as much as Swedes did. In marketing terms, one is selling the sizzle, not the steak, that is, associating a measure with attractions unrelated to its substance.

Symbols invite responses based on the overall positive or negative image of a country without regard to programme details. Throughout the world, the United States is a strong symbol, albeit one that can convey negative as well as positive responses. It has more positive associations in Britain and less in France. The United States can also provoke divisive responses within a country. In a patronizing manner, elites may dismiss a programme encouraging the spread of cheap retail chain stores as leading to the 'McDonaldization' of its marketplace, while ordinary citizens who patronize McDonald's when shopping may welcome more cheap chain stores.

Within Europe, Germany has long been a strong and ambiguous symbol. For the oldest generation, the experience of occupation by Nazi Germany during the Second World War can remain powerful. The median European was born two decades later, when West Germany had become a model economy combining a high rate of growth, full employment, and low inflation. Moreover, the social market ideology of its Christian Democratic and Social Democratic governments had a broad ideological appeal to continental Europeans. Since the fall of the Berlin Wall, the economic slowdown in Germany has made it a much less attractive symbol in Western Europe, while its historic economic achievements remain positively attractive in post-Communist countries trying to reconstruct their economies. In Washington, the German government's refusal to support American action against Iraq has made Germany a symbol of effete, 'old' Europe.

The partisan complexion of government affects its symbolic appeal. For any party in opposition, a party of the same broad political colour in power elsewhere is an appealing symbol of electoral success. In opposition, intellectuals in the British Labour Party have often looked to Sweden's social democratic government, although in office Labour governments have usually aovided copying Swedish programmes that provide a high level of benefits at the cost of high taxes. When a Democrat, Jimmy Carter, was president and Conservative Margaret Thatcher was prime minister, American Republicans looked to Downing Street rather than to the White House for symbolic gratification.

British media outlets, and especially the tabloid press, glory in headlines that display extreme xenophobia, dismissing the French as 'frog-eaters' and describing Germans in terms reflecting Adolf Hitler's legacy. By contrast, the media read by policymakers, such *The Economist* and *Financial Times*, are cosmopolitan in outlook and sell as many copies outside Britain as within it.

If policymakers do not actively sell a lesson, then whatever its merits in theory it will never leave the drawing board. Because marketing emphasizes symbols, it appeals to what is fashionable. While invoking a fashionable country can be useful in promoting a lesson, symbols are empty of specific content. A symbol must support a programme that sets out actions for government to take if it is not to suffer the fate of transitory fashions that are discarded soon after they catch the public's eye.

Some things that can be done to increase a programme's prospects for success are in the hands of the designers of the programme, for example, keeping goals clear and cause-and-effect relationships simple. There are other things that the proponents of a programme can do to try to increase its prospects when bargaining for the political commitment necessary to secure adoption, for example, offering concessions that are substantively or symbolically important to critics but that do not result in the crippling of a programme. However much effort is invested in controlling the promotion of a lesson, there is one thing that policymakers cannot control: the future.

Step 10
Looking ahead

Efforts to generate learning within an organization have no conclusion. There is no finish line.
Ray C. Rist, 'The Preconditions for Learning'

Any suggestion to introduce a new programme invites the challenge: what would happen if it were adopted? The straightforward way to resolve such a debate is to introduce it and learn after the fact whether supporters or opponents are correct about its consequences. In business, feedback from the marketplace is often used to find out what customers will buy. A fashion merchant can try out new lines of clothing, aiming to make enough profits on the fashions that sell to offset losses on those that are remaindered. However, it is much more difficult for a government to get rid of programmes that have no appeal to citizens. It cannot offer a one-third reduction in taxes if citizens will accept public services that nobody else wants. Even if policymakers write off a new programme as part of a process of learning from experience, voters can punish them for their mistakes.

The primary demand of policymakers is not for after-the-fact evaluation of what they have done; it is for prospective evaluation, that is, a before-the-fact forecast about whether a proposed programme will succeed or fail. If a proposal simply modifies an existing programme, there is evidence at hand that can be used to forecast the effect of change. For example, the impact of an increase in a tax on tobacco can be calculated as a function of the extra revenue per pound of tobacco sold, less the reduction in tobacco use due to the price increase and due to the smuggling of tobacco from lower-tax jurisdictions.

Standard forecasting methods cannot be used, however, to make a prospective evaluation of a novel programme, since there is not yet a stream of evidence about its performance. Some politicians welcome this, for the absence of evidence removes all bounds on speculation. It is left to the imagination of politicians interested in marketing or vetoing a proposal to pronounce on its consequences.

Confronted with uncertainties, cautious policymakers prefer the known difficulties of the status quo to the risks of adopting a new programme. Yet to assume the continuation of current levels of satisfaction is itself a forecast about the future. As time goes by, changes in society will cause the consequences of a programme to change, especially if the programme itself is left unaltered. In a complementary manner, if a new programme is adopted, policymakers will gain lots of evidence about its consequences and can use this feedback to modify their original design to increase satisfaction. As the epigraph to this chapter emphasizes, policymakers need to be continuously open to learning about the programmes for which they are responsible.

Lesson-drawing makes it possible to put bounds on speculation. As the first section of this chapter reminds us, while a proposal based on a foreign model has no domestic track record, it does offer evidence of what a programme achieves abroad. While this cannot demonstrate what would happen if it were imported here, it does place bounds on the speculative claims of a proposal's proponents and opponents. Professionals can use the evidence to simulate a range of prospective evaluations. Yet even the most careful of bounded evaluations is still only a forecast of what might happen.

The adoption of a lesson creates a radically different situation. Instead of speculating about what might happen, policymakers can learn from the feedback that the new measure generates. As the second section emphasizes, learning from feedback is an evolutionary process. The introduction of a new programme changes politics: the goal is now sustainability and a new measure creates new supporters. However, political support does not guarantee successful routinization, for changes in society can force alterations in a programme or even its abandonment. The conclusion of the book emphasizes that, while politicians may live in a world of now or never, new programmes emerge through a sooner-or-later process. The uncertainties of politics are a reminder that policymakers cannot determine that a lesson will never be applied, yet they also mean that promoters of a new lesson may have to wait a long time before a window of opportunity opens.

Evaluation – prospective and retrospective

An evaluation can focus on what has happened in the more or less recent past, or else it can be directed at what may happen in future. There is often lots of evidence available to make retrospective judgements. Historians can extend evaluation for a century or more in order to identify both the intended and the unintended consequences of past choices, such as the English Repeal of the Corn Laws in 1846 or Abraham Lincoln's emancipation of black slaves in 1863. By contrast, evidence of the future will only become available well beyond the time horizon of the politicians, for whom the date of the next election, or even a week is the cut-off point for their attention.

Whereas the past is given, the future is open. Policymakers know this, for they must make choices today that influence what happens in future. For that reason, there is a demand for prospective evaluations that try to assess what would happen *if* a lesson were adopted, an existing programme kept, or nothing done in the hope that current dissatisfaction would go away. Because the future has not yet happened, the lack of evidence encourages unbounded speculation. However, when a new programme is based on a lesson from abroad, then speculation is bounded because it is evidence-based.

Evaluation through the rear-view mirror

The starting point for a historian is the identification of events in the past. Written records are assiduously searched to build up an account of past circumstances. Often, the events written about – the English Civil War, the French Revolution, or the Great Society of Lyndon Johnson – were controversial in their time and can still stir political passions today.

The way in which historians interpret sources depends not only on what is in written records but also what is in the historian's mind, his or her theoretical ideas and 'feel' for the period. Because historical interpretations and, even more, inferences for the present drawn from the past are conjectural, they are often disputed among historians. While historians can supply today's policymakers with analogies to use as ammunition in political debate, their 'thick' descriptions of past events are not the base for forecasting the future.

The textbook method of social science evaluation views programmes through a rear-view mirror, but the time horizon is usually much shorter than a historian's, because of demands that today's programmes be evaluated on the basis of readily available statistical evidence. Typically, evaluation takes the form of the analysis of quantitative data about programme inputs and outputs, for example, the amount of money spent, the number of individuals or organizations dealt with, and so forth. The most prolific sources of data are likely to be the administrative records of the agency conducting the programme. This may be supplemented with some data about outcomes, that is, whether or not the intended targets of a programme are or are not better off, whatever the cause.

In the simplest form, programme outputs and inputs can be related in order to arrive at a cost/benefit or cost/effectiveness ratio. Such an analysis indicates how much 'bang for the buck' a programme produces. An input/output evaluation has a better grounding in evidence than assertions by self-interested politicians. However, it gives a static picture of a programme.

A trend analysis can be undertaken when a programme has persisted for years, in order to evaluate whether its performance is steady, improving, or deteriorating. Since collecting official data and statistical analysis both require time, a trend analysis is usually a year or more out of date. It can be used for evidence-based speculation by projecting a trend forward to forecast future performance. However, any projection must always bear the qualification 'all other conditions remaining constant'. This condition applies only if both a programme and its intended targets remain static.

Evaluations are most needed when there are palpable signs that all other conditions are not constant. For example, economic forecasts cannot simply project past trends forward because the economy is in a state of continuous flux, resulting in growth, inflation, and unemployment rates changing direction from year to year, sometimes going down and sometimes up. When signs of political dissatisfaction arise, policymakers do not want conditions to remain constant, but the downward trend in a programme to be stopped and then reversed by the adoption of a new programme.

Prospective evaluation – with and without evidence

Since no evidence is available that can be used to prove or disprove claims about the future, politicians can treat it as a form of silly putty, moulding it into whatever shape suits their purpose. Instead of evidence, assumptions can be postulated that will justify any conclusion desired. Proponents of a new programme can reason from one implausible premise to another or abandon logic entirely in order to assert claims of unbounded success.

In the absence of evidence, the distinction between what is possible and what is desirable is obliterated (see Box 8.5). Uncertainties about the future offer politicians opportunities to use their imagination to proclaim an appealing but vague vision of a brighter future if a programme is adopted. If doubts are voiced, faith in the governing party can be invoked or a politician can simply urge, 'Trust me.' Those who show a lack of faith and persist in questioning whether the good intentions of government are enough to guarantee success run the risk of being marginalized or excluded from future discussions of policy.

In the absence of evidence, political opponents are free to speculate about dire consequences if a new measure is adopted. Unbounded speculation can turn into a battle of political wills. Politicians regard 'will' as a positive virtue; it is the expression of an individual's power to force policy preferences on others. Margaret Thatcher is a classic example of a politician determined to ignore forecasts of defeat or disaster. As prime minister, she 'willed' programmes that turned out to be successful, such as laws requiring free and fair trade union ballots on strikes and on the election of union officials. But other measures turned out to be wilful in the negative sense, such as an ideologically determined programme to finance local government through a flat-rate poll tax on local citizens.

Lesson-drawing offers evidence for the evaluation of a programme, since its starting point is the examination of a programme already in operation in another country. While a lesson drawn from a foreign example has more unfamiliar elements than a home-grown measure, the provision of vicarious evidence places bounds on speculation. A ceiling is imposed on expectations, inasmuch as a programme adapted from a foreign example is unlikely to produce better results than its original. Furthermore, the discipline involved in creating a model focuses attention on cause-and-effect relationships essential in making a programme effective.

Implementation analysis and prospective evaluation are both means of accident prevention. They turn the spotlight on elements of a programme that have not been thought about and that threaten failure if something is not done. The identification of shortcomings in advance makes it possible to remedy faults before they occur rather than face embarrassment after a programme is put into effect. Implementation analysis focuses on what public officials need to do to get a programme started. Since it emphasizes the difficulty of doing anything for the first time, implementation analysis thus puts brakes on unbounded speculations of policymakers, who are ready to take credit for a new programme before it has been put into effect (Pressman and Wildavsky, 1973). Prospective evaluation goes further: it is concerned with what happens after a programme is implemented. If most of its consequences appear negative, prospective evaluation can lead to the conclusion that a lesson that initially appears attractive because successful elsewhere should not be introduced here.

The British government's attempt to improve the skills of young workers by introducing a programme using Germany's system of vocational training as a model illustrates how prospective evaluation can prove valuable. The starting point of the German vocational training model is a solid foundation in the national language, mathematics, a foreign language, and at least two other subjects. Under the German dual system, German youths combine part-time education in relevant vocational subjects, such as chemistry for dry cleaners or animal hygiene for butchers, with on-the-job training as an apprentice assigned to a *Meister*, a senior employee respected by fellow workers because of his or her skills and commitment to teaching their trade to apprentices. As an adult, the *Meister* is a role model and mentor to youths in their first job (Hamilton, 1990). At the end of two or three years, the apprentice must pass a national examination that combines written tests in relevant skills with the practical demonstration of the ability to do whatever his or her occupation requires, such as bake and decorate a cake. The programme attracted British policymakers because, by the age of twenty, most young Germans have learned the difference between being in school with other teenagers and working in an adult environment, as well as having a vocational qualification and a foundation for learning on the job as work requirements change.

Before the British government implemented its 'German-style' vocational training system in the late 1980s, I undertook a prospective evaluation of its likely outcome that identified two fundamental weaknesses (Rose and Wignanek, 1990). First, the majority of British youths leaving school for work at sixteen did not have levels of literacy and numeracy high enough to benefit from vocational training at the German standard. For this reason, the prospective evaluation forecast that many youths entering the new British system would achieve only a 'dumbed-down' qualification, or drop out of a training system that was not compulsory. This happened. Second, there was absent in the British labour force workers like the German *Meister*, people who were both good at the job and committed to training youths. Thus, good on-the-job practical training was lacking. Because the British system sought to achieve training without trainers, it was doomed to failure. A decade and a half after the attempt to emulate Germany's programme of vocational education, the prime minister's Strategy Unit labelled British vocational education a failure.

While retrospective and prospective evaluation can each identify causes of failure, their instrumental value is very different. Retrospective evaluation explains what went wrong after the fact, that is, when it is too late for policy-makers to do anything, except admit their mistake or shift the blame to others. By contrast, prospective evaluation is an early warning system about the risk of failure. For those committed to making a new programme work, the identi-fication of obstacles and risks through prospective evaluation highlights steps that can be taken now to produce success in future. If nothing can be done to rectify shortcomings, it is an argument for not applying a lesson, however attractive it may appear from a distance. For example, if British policymakers had invested less effort in promising to produce a German-style vocational qualification and more in improving basic education for non-academic youths and a cadre of master workers who could become trainers in future, there would be a more skilled British labour force today.

As time goes by: evolution and adaptation

Politicians prefer to deal with issues that are in the headlines today rather than applying themselves to the continuous monitoring and evaluation of programmes that have already been adopted. President Lyndon Johnson focused his attention on getting Congress to adopt new programmes. Once he had signed a Great Society measure into law at an impressive White House ceremony, Johnson turned his attention to securing another piece of Great Society legislation with little regard to how his previous legislative achievements were working in practice.

Whereas the formal enactment of a new programme is a specific event that can be celebrated with a bill-signing ceremony at the White House or television coverage, the evolution of a programme is a time-consuming process that involves hard work with little publicity. Even the best of prospective evaluations cannot anticipate everything that happens as time goes by. Every new pro-gramme has unforeseen consequences, and this is especially true of lessons from abroad, since their greater novelty makes their effects harder to predict than the modification of an established domestic programme.

Once a lesson is implemented, a lesson is no longer a foreign import; instead, its evolution is now an integral part of the dynamics of national society and politics. When feedback shows that a programme works differently in practice than on the drawing board, policymakers must make adaptations. With the passage of time, both the programme and its political support alter.

Changing programmes changes politics

The adoption of a lesson radically alters its political situation. It is no longer meaningful to debate what might happen if a lesson is applied here. Nor is it necessary to evaluate its effects through a foreign lens; they can now be seen close at hand. The programme is no longer a speculative idea challenging the status quo; instead, it is an accomplished fact.

At its launch, the sustainability of a new programme is a goal, not a certainty (Patashnik, 2003: 208ff.). The political challenge to reformers who have seen their lesson adopted is to hold on to what they have won rather than see it undermined by opponents and neglected by its sponsors. In defence of a new programme, its proponents enjoy the resources of government.

The surest way to protect a new programme from falling victim to counter-attack by its opponents is to abolish the institutions that are their power base. This was the hallmark of the privatization of state-owned British enterprises undertaken by Margaret Thatcher and of many programmes that drew lessons from that initiative. Shifting the ownership of industries from state to private hands was opposed by leaders of state-owned enterprise and trade unions representing employees. Once an industry was sold to the private sector, the directors of state-owned enterprises lost their power base. They faced the choice of competing to hold their post in what was now a profit-making company, finding a job elsewhere, or going into retirement. Similarly, the Thatcher government's privatization of housing owned by local government was implemented by selling houses at deeply discounted prices to their tenants. Thus, any proposal to rena-tionalize housing would have been strongly resisted by the new owners and the cost of renationalizing housing at market prices would have been far greater than the capital gained by selling the houses.

A new programme creates new interests that will want to see it sustained. Electoral reform is a classic example of this happening. When a proposal to alter electoral rules is brought up, many elected under the established system will oppose it root-and-branch. Yet as and when election laws are changed, officeholders must accept the new system and make it work to their advantage if they want to retain their political position, or leave electoral politics altogether. In New Zealand a combination of events led to a national referendum in 1993 that mandated the replacement of its British-style electoral system with a mixed member system with a substantial proportional representation element. New Zealand politicians responded to the new law by forming new parties and the result was anticipated by prospective evaluation: an increase in the number of parties winning seats and government by coalition. In turn, coalition govern-ment led to rancorous disputes between politicians and instability in parties unpopular with the electorate. While politicians elected by the new system do not want to repeal it, New Zealand reformers now are once again searching abroad, looking for lessons from European countries about how to combine coalition government and stable, consensual government (see Boston, 1998).

Social change changes programmes

A new programme is intended to produce a visible change in society, either making conditions better or at least removing political dissatisfaction. But it is shortsighted for policymakers to think that the decisions they take are the only cause of changes in society. From a sociological perspective, the introduction of a new programme is but one input to the continuing evolution of society. While some changes can be anticipated, others cannot.

When making a prospective evaluation, policy analysts calculate the probable changes that a programme will introduce in its target environment. But the outcome of a programme depends not only on how it is designed and implemented, but also on what is happening within society. Furthermore, the results of intermestic programmes are affected by what happens in other societies and in the international economy as well as by what is done by a particular government department. For example, if a new youth employment programme is launched when a world recession is starting, youth unemployment is bound to rise. Even if careful analysis indicates that the rise is less than would otherwise have been the case, the government's new programme is vulnerable to attack for failing to reverse the tide. Alternatively, if a new employment programme is introduced when the international economy is about to boom, it will appear successful, even if its contribution to rising employment is slight compared to the impact of expanding demand at home and abroad.

Since programmes are usually targeted at relatively limited segments of the population, the social conditions relevant to a new programme may be static or changing. If relevant conditions are static, then the satisfaction or dissatisfaction that feeds back to policymakers will very much be determined by the care or lack of care that went into its design. However, if social conditions are changing, the net effect can either reinforce the extent of satisfaction that a programme generates, or be a more important influence on feedback from the programme than the programme design. Since feedback reflects the combined influence of social conditions and programme characteristics, the response of policymakers can take four different forms (Box 10.1).

The goal in introducing a new programme is not only to dispel dissatisfaction but to sustain satisfaction. If this happens, then the programme can *run by routine*. The intended beneficiaries will be content and busy policymakers can then turn their attention to other fires in their in-trays. However, routinization requires not only the careful drawing and implementation of a lesson, but also social conditions to remain stable.

Box 10.1 Political responses to feedback from society

Society

	Changes	Static
Programme feedback		
Satisfaction	CLAIM FRESH CREDIT	ROUTINIZE
Dissatisfaction	ADAPT	RECONSTRUCT, ABANDON

Because social changes take many forms, it is possible for changing conditions to have a positive effect on a lesson. For example, if a programme is introduced to help members of low-income groups buy homes, and changes in the international economy lead to a fall in interest rates, this will make interest rates and mortgage payments fall, thereby having a positive effect on satisfaction with the housing programme. For politicians, the extent to which satisfaction is due to circumstances outside their control is politically irrelevant. The immediately important point is that the success of the new programme is increased and politicians can *claim fresh credit*.

If a lesson produces political dissatisfaction without any change in society, then it is difficult for policymakers to explain away its faults by blaming international conditions or unexpected events. The immediate priority is to *reconstruct* the programme in order to remove the causes of dissatisfaction. A re-examination of foreign experience can be helpful, if it shows that the problems faced are similar to the teething problems that had been faced by the original programme long before it was viewed by visitors. If neither a return to foreign examples or a close examination of a new programme points to actions that can be taken to get rid of a rising tide of dissatisfaction with a new measure, then the political line of least resistance is to *abandon* it.

Dissatisfaction from changes in society tests the flexibility of a new programme. Whereas it can take years before changes in society cause political aggravation, a new programme is more likely to generate negative feedback within a matter of months of its impact being felt. When dissatisfaction with an established programme is voiced, the instinct of policymakers is to defend it as a temporary problem caused by events. However, when changes in society are associated with a new programme, then policymakers have less reason to leave it as it is and good cause to *adapt* the programme in an effort to remedy its defects and dispel dissatisfaction.

Never say never in politics – but you may have to wait

The time horizons of politicians differ, and with them their readiness to think about introducing long-term changes in public policy. When Winston Churchill became prime minister of Great Britain at a time of crisis in 1940, he not only told Parliament that he had 'nothing to offer but blood, toil, tears, and sweat' but also cautioned that the road to victory would be 'long and hard'. When Margaret Thatcher became prime minister in 1979, she had a lengthy list of programmes that she wanted to introduce to change the direction of British government. When some caused political controversy and she was urged to change course, she remained committed to long-term change, making a pun on the title of a well-known English play, 'The lady's not for turning.' The proof of her achievement is not only in the programmes introduced before she left office in 1990 but also in those introduced by her successors of different parties, John Major and Tony Blair.

'Nowness' is a characteristic of many politicians today. The date of the next election is the furthest limit of their time horizon. Politicians focus immediately on media deadlines. When weekly periodicals were important political vehicles of political communication, Prime Minister Harold Wilson coined the phrase, 'A week in politics is a long time.' The acceleration and expansion of the media since has shortened the time horizon of media-conscious politicians to less than twenty-four hours. The day starts with morning news and newspapers and ends with late-night bulletins on television, radio, and the Internet. This leaves little or no time for learning about programmes abroad and reflecting on whether or how they could be applied at home.

When a politician who lives for 'now' says that a lesson can never be applied, this means it is politically out of the question for the moment. But momentary objections are, by definition, transitory. This makes today's objection variable across time. A politician who lives for the present can ignore this fact, but it cannot be ignored in the study of political change. An extreme example of long-term change is the introduction of decimal currency in Britain (Box 10.2).

Paradoxically, the more importance that is attributed to 'now', the greater the degree of openness that is introduced into politics, for 'nowness' implies that, just because a lesson is politically unacceptable or technically unfeasible today, that is no reason to assume that it will not be acceptable tomorrow. The transitoriness of obstacles to change is especially relevant when an election looms, for measures that were politically unacceptable the day before an election can, if there is a change of government, be high-priority items the day after a new government is sworn into office. However, many programme changes do not occur so dramatically nor is change confined solely to elections.

Policy innovations occur in two contrasting time scales. Some changes are the consequence of a lengthy and cumulative process of deliberation in which

---

Box 10.2 Long-term policy change: decimalization of currency in England

- First to third centuries AD. Coins were circulating in England when the Roman army occupied England.
- Eighth century. The pound became a recognized currency with a value of 240 pennies.
- Eighth to seventeenth centuries. Gradual development of a currency based on 4 farthings equal to 1 penny; 12 pennies equal to 1 shilling; and 20 shillings equal to £1.
- Eighteenth century. Proponents of the Enlightenment in Britain and France promoted decimalization for currency, weights, and measures. While France adopted decimal measures, in England the war with Napoleon discouraged following the French example.
- 1816. First debate in Parliament on the decimalization of currency.
- 1971. Introduction of decimal currency in which 100 pence equals one pound.

Source: See Arnold-Baker, 1996 328ff.

---

policymakers puzzle over anomalies in existing programmes and, free from intense pressures for immediate action, finally introduce improvements (Heclo, 1974). Other changes are abrupt, occurring when events create so much dissatisfaction that the demand for a new programme forces policymakers to do something even when they have not had time to consider what to do (cf. Polsby, 1984).

While initial welfare state programmes may have been modelled on a pioneering programme in another country, their evolution over the past century has involved incremental changes expanding coverage and improving the level of benefits. However, events have created crises, most notably the fiscal problems of the 1970s, when public expenditure zoomed upwards while tax revenues fell as national economies contracted. In Britain, a Labour government was forced by escalating public deficits and inflation to slam the brakes on spending. In the 1980s, both Margaret Thatcher and Ronald Reagan won elections by promoting programmes to reduce public spending, cutting taxes, privatizing publicly owned firms, and stressing market principles. Their ideologically fuelled responses to fiscal crisis have since provided lessons to governors across many continents.

In the fullness of time, a country that was once an importer of lessons from abroad can become an exporter, or vice versa. In the past century and a half, Japan has gone through multiple role reversals (Box 10.3). The appearance of American gunboats in Yokohama in 1854 was the initial stimulus for an isolated island state to learn from the West or risk becoming its subservient colony. Radical domestic changes in constitutional structures were paralleled by sending

---

Box 10.3 Japan: reversing roles in lesson-drawing

- 1854. Japan opened up to the West after American naval officer Matthew C. Perry sailed steamboats armed with cannons into Tokyo Bay.
- 1868. Meiji regime established. Japanese government begins sending officials to Europe to learn how to modernize.
- 1905. Japan wins its first war fought by modern means, the Russo-Japanese war.
- 1922. Recognition of Japan as a major Asian power when it becomes the co-signator, with the United States and Britain, of a treaty to limit naval power.
- 1937. Japan invades China and conquers large areas.
- 1940. Japan forms an Axis with Hitler's Germany and Mussolini's Italy, a military alliance dividing territory for conquest in the Second World War.
- 1941. Japan attacks the United States at Pearl Harbor.
- 1945. Unconditional surrender of Japan immediately after two atom bombs dropped on the country. United States military occupation follows.
- 1947. A new Japanese constitution adopted that is democratic in form. American diplomat John Foster Dulles dismisses the Japanese economy as fit only to export cheap trinkets to Woolworths.
- 1970s–1980s. Enormous growth in the quantity and quality of Japanese exports such as automobiles and consumer electronics. Western businessmen and academics come to Japan to seek lessons from Japanese manufacturers.
- 1990s–2000+. Slowdown and stagnation of Japanese economy lead Western government to examine Japan for lessons in how not to manage an economy.

Japanese public officials to Europe to learn how to introduce a modern postal service and create a modern army (Westney, 1987). By the first quarter of the twentieth century, Japan had learned sufficient lessons to establish military equality with the West. After being defeated in the Second World War, Japan then sought lessons in industrialization. Within a generation, Japanese products were selling well on world markets. The success of Japanese industry was held up as an example from which Western governments could learn. However, in the 1990s, the Japanese economy began to stagnate, and today Western governments wanting to avoid an economy in which costs are high and growth is low can study Japan in order to learn what not to do.

Timing is critical for adopting a lesson from abroad. Whatever the quality of the evidence and reasoning in favour of applying a lesson, nothing will happen as long as citizens are satisfied and governors have no motive to depart from the status quo. Advocates of new programmes must wait for a conjuncture of events to make change possible. In the words of an American lobbyist:

> When you lobby for something, what you have to do is put together your coalition, and then you sit there and wait for the fortuitous event.

As I see it, people who are trying to advocate change are like surfers waiting for the big wave. You get out there, you have to be ready to go, you have to be ready to paddle. If you're not ready to paddle when the big wave comes along, you're not going to ride it in.

(Quoted in Kingdon, 1984: 171)

Sooner or later, a big wave does come along – but not every advocate of a lesson has the patience to wait for this to happen. Yet the time that programme advocates spend waiting need not be wasted. Policymakers committed to improving public programmes rather than to making headlines and careers can use the time made available by their lack of influence to learn more about programmes relevant to future action. In that way, they can be better informed about what lessons to draw from abroad when the window of opportunity opens.

In the first instance, success is registered when what can be learned abroad becomes the basis for an innovative programme nationally. As a new programme evolves, it will be adapted to fit better into its national context. As time goes by, the ultimate achievement is that the foreign origins of a programme are forgotten. It then becomes described as no more and no less than 'the way we do things here'.

References

Anderson, Charles, 1978. 'The Logic of Public Problems'. In Douglas Ashford, ed., *Comparing Public Policies*. Beverly Hills: Sage, 19–42.

Argyris, Chris, 1982. *Reasoning, Learning and Action*. San Francisco: Jossey-Bass.

Arnold-Baker, Charles, 1996. *The Companion to British History*. Tunbridge Wells, Kent: Longcross Press.

Bache, Ian and Olsson, J., 2001. 'Legitimacy through Partnership? EU Policy Diffusion in Britain and Sweden', *Scandinavian Political Studies*, 24, 3, 215–237.

Bache, Ian and Taylor, Andrew, 2003. 'The Politics of Policy Resistance: Reconstructing Higher Education in Kosovo', *Journal of Public Policy*, 23, 3, 279–300.

Black, John, 1997. *Oxford Dictionary of Economics*. Oxford: Oxford University Press.

Boston, Jonathan, 1998. *Governing under Proportional Representation: Lessons from Europe*. Wellington, New Zealand: Institute of Policy Studies.

Cain, Piers, 1999. 'Automating Personnel Records for Improved Management of Human Resources'. In Richard Heeks, ed., *Reinventing Government in the Information Age*. London: Routledge, 135–155.

Casey, Bernard H. and Gold, Michael, 2004. 'Peer Review of Labour Market Policies in the European Union'. London: Birkbeck College, duplicated.

Council of State Governments, 1990. *The Book of the States*. Lexington, KY: Council of State Governments.

Cowles, Maria Green, Caporaso, James and Risse, Thomas, 2003. *Transforming Europe: Europeanization and Domestic Change*. Ithaca, NY: Cornell University Press.

Cyert, R. and March, J.G., 1963. *A Behavioral Theory of the Firm*. Englewood Cliffs, NJ: Prentice-Hall.

David, Paul A., 1985. 'Clio and the Economics of QWERTY', *American Economic Review*, 75, 2, 332–337.

Deutsch, Karl W., 1963. *The Nerves of Government*. New York: Free Press.

Dewar, James A., 2002. *Assumption-Based Planning: A Tool for Reducing Avoidable Surprises*. New York: Cambridge University Press.

Dolowitz, David and Marsh, David, 1996. 'Who Learns What from Whom: A Review of the Policy Transfer Literature', *Political Studies*, 44, 343–357.

Enterprise Directorate-General, 2002. *Improving Trans-national Policy Learning in Innovation*. Luxembourg: Innovation–SME Programme report of Réné Wintjes.

Finer, Catherine Jones, ed., 2003. *Social Policy Reform in China: Views from Home and Abroad*. Aldershot: Ashgate.

Grabbe, Heather, 2002. 'European Union Conditionality and the *Acquis Communautaire*', *International Political Science Review*, 23, 3, 249–268.

Haas, Ernst, 1990. *When Knowledge Is Power: Three Models of Choice in International Organizations*. Berkeley: University of California Press.

Hamilton, Stephen F., 1990. *Apprenticeship for Adulthood*. New York: Free Press.

Heclo, Hugh, 1974. *Modern Social Politics in Britain and Sweden*. New Haven: Yale University Press.

Hemmer, Christopher R., 2000. *Which Lessons Matter? American Foreign Policy Decision-making in the Middle East, 1979–1987*. Albany: SUNY Press.

Henig, J.R., Hammett, C. and Feigenbaum, H.B., 1988. 'The Politics of Privatization: A Comparative Perspective', *Governance*, 1, 442–468.

Hirsch, Fred, 1977. *Social Limits to Growth*. London: Routledge.

Hirschman, Albert O., 1973. *Journeys toward Progress: Studies of Economic Policy-Making in Latin America*. New York: Twentieth Century Fund.

Hoberg, George, 1991. 'Sleeping with an Elephant: The American Influence on Canadian Environmental Legislation', *Journal of Public Policy*, 11, 1, 107–132.

Holliday, Ian, 2000. 'Productivist Welfare Capitalism: Social Policy in East Asia', *Political Studies*, 48, 706–723.

Hood, Christopher, Rothstein, Henry and Baldwin, Robert, 2001. *The Government of Risk*. Oxford: Oxford University Press.

Inglehart, R., Basanez, M. and Moreno, A., 1998. *Human Values and Beliefs: A Cross-Cultural Sourcebook*. Ann Arbor: University of Michigan Press.

Issing, Ottmar, Gaspar, V., Angeloni, I. and Tristani, O., 2001. *Monetary Policy in the Euro Area: Strategy and Decision-Making in the European Central Bank*. Cambridge: Cambridge University Press.

Jacoby, Wade, 2000. *Imitation and Politics: Redesigning Modern Germany*. Ithaca, NY: Cornell University Press.

Jacoby, Wade, 2001. 'Tutors and Pupils: International Organizations, Central European Elites and Western Models', *Governance*, 14, 2, 169–200.

Johnstone, Dorothy, 1975. *A Tax Shall Be Charged*. London: Civil Service Studies, Her Majesty's Stationery Office.

Jönsson, Christer, Tägil, Sven and Törnqvist, Gunnar, 2000. *Organizing European Space*. London: Sage.

Keck, Margaret E. and Sikkink, Kathryn, 1998. *Activists beyond Borders: Advocacy Networks in International Politics*. Ithaca, NY: Cornell University Press.

Khanna, V.R., 1991. 'Economists Discuss Eastern Europe, Uruguay Round and European Monetary Union', *IMF Survey*, 30 September, 277–280.

Khong, Yuen Foon, 1992. *Analogies at War: Korea, Dien Bien Phu and the Vietnam Decisions of 1965*. Princeton: Princeton University Press.

Kingdon, John W., 1984. *Agendas, Alternatives and Public Policies*. Boston: Little, Brown.

Kingdon, John W., 1998. *America the Unusual*. New York: St Martin's Press.

Knill, Christoph, 2001. *The Europeanisation of National Administrations*. Cambridge: Cambridge University Press.

Leppard, David, 2003. 'Blair Gets Gas-Proof Armoured Jaguar', *Sunday Times*, 9 March.

Lindblom, C.E., 1965. *The Intelligence of Democracy*. New York: Free Press.

Lipset, S.M., 1996. *American Exceptionalism: A Double-Edged Sword*. New York: W.W. Norton.

Luce, Edward, 2003. 'US Seeks Indian Advice on Preventing Power Blackouts', *Financial Times*, 30 August.

Lundvall, Bengt-Ake and Tomlinson, Mark, 2002. 'International Benchmarking as a Policy Learning Tool'. In Maria João Rodrigues, ed., *The New Knowledge Economy in Europe*. Cheltenham: Edward Elgar, 203–231.

McDonald's Corporation, 2003a. *Financial Report 2002*. Oak Park, IL: McDonald's Corporation.

McDonald's Corporation, 2003b. *Summary Annual Report 2002*. Oak Park, IL: McDonald's Corporation.

Mossberger, Karen A., 2000. *The Politics of Ideas and the Spread of Enterprise Zones*. Washington, DC: Georgetown University Press.

Mossberger, Karen and Hale, Kathleen, 2002. 'Polydiffusion in Intergovernmental Programs', *American Review of Public Administration*, 32, 4, 398–422.

Neustadt, Richard E. and May, Ernest R., 1986. *Thinking in Time: The Uses of History for Decision-Makers*. New York: Free Press.

North, Douglass C., 1990. *Institutions, Institutional Change and Economic Performance*. New York: Cambridge University Press.

Nugent, Neill, 1994. *The Government and Politics of the European Union*. London: Macmillan, 3rd edition.

Nye, Joseph S. Jr., 2002. *The Paradox of American Power*. New York: Oxford University Press.

Oates, Stephen B., 1982. *Let the Trumpet Sound*. New York: Harper & Row.

Olsen, Johan P. and Peters, B. Guy, 1996. *Lessons from Experience: Experiential Learning in Administrative Reforms in Eight Democracies*. Oslo: Scandinavian University Press.

Patashnik, Eric, 2003. 'After the Public Interest Prevails: The Political Sustainability of Policy Reform', *Governance*, 16, 2, 203–234.

Pickel, Andreas, 1997. 'The Jump-Started Economy and the Ready-Made State: A Theoretical Reconsideration of the East German Case', *Comparative Political Studies*, 30, 2, April, 211–241.

Pierson, Paul, 2000. 'Increasing Returns, Path Dependence and the Study of Politics', *American Political Science Review*, 94, 2, 251–268.

Polsby, Nelson, 1984. *Policy Innovation in America*. New Haven: Yale University Press.

de la Porte, Catherine, Pochet, Philippe and Room, Graham, 2001. 'Social Benchmarking, Policymaking and New Governance in the European Union', *Journal of European Social Policy*, 11, 4, 291–307.

Pressman, Jeffrey and Wildavsky, Aaron, 1973. *Implementation*. Berkeley: University of California Press.

Rist, Ray C., 1994. 'The Preconditions for Learning'. In F.L. Leeuw, R.C. Rist and R.C. Sonnichsen, eds., *Can Governments Learn?* New Brunswick, NJ: Transaction Publishers, 189–206.

Rogers, Everett M., 1995. *Diffusion of Innovations*. New York: Free Press, 4th edition.

Rose, Richard, ed., 1974. *Lessons from America: An Exploration*. London: Macmillan.

Rose, Richard, 1985. 'The Programme Approach to the Growth of Government', *British Journal of Political Science*, 15, 1, 1–18.

Rose, Richard, 1986. 'Common Goals but Different Roles: The State's Contribution to the Welfare Mix'. In R. Rose and Rei Shiratori, eds., *The Welfare State East and West*. New York: Oxford University Press, 13–39.

Rose, Richard, 1988. 'The Growth of Government Organizations: Do We Count the Number or Weigh the Programs?' In C. Campbell and B.G. Peters, eds., *Organizing Governance, Governing Organizations*. Pittsburgh: University of Pittsburgh Press, 99–128.

Rose, Richard, 1991a. 'Is American Public Policy Exceptional?' In Byron Shafer, ed., *Is America Different?* New York: Oxford University Press, 187–229.

Rose, Richard, 1991b. 'Prospective Evaluation through Comparative Analysis'. In Paul Ryan, ed., *International Comparisons of Vocational Education and Training.* London: Falmer Press, 68–92.

Rose, Richard, 1993. *Lesson-Drawing in Public Policy: A Guide to Learning across Time and Space.* Chatham, NJ: Chatham House.

Rose, Richard, 1996. *What Is Europe? A Dynamic Perspective.* New York and London: Longman.

Rose, Richard, ed., 2000. *The International Encyclopedia of Elections.* Washington, DC: CQ Press.

Rose, Richard, 2002. 'Economies In Transformation: A Multidimensional Approach to a Cross-Cultural Problem', *East European Constitutional Review*, 11, 4/12, 1, 62–70.

Rose, Richard, 2003a. 'What's Wrong with Best Practice Policies and Why Relevant Practices Are Better'. In House of Commons Public Administration Select Committee, *On Target? Government By Measurement.* London: The Stationery Office, Ltd. HC 62-II, Ev 308–317.

Rose, Richard, 2003b. 'When All Other Conditions Are Not Equal: The Context for Drawing Lessons'. In Finer, 2003, 5–22.

Rose, Richard and Davies, Phillip, 1994. *Inheritance in Public Policy: Change without Choice in Britain.* New Haven: Yale University Press.

Rose, Richard and Wignanek, Günter, 1990. *Training without Trainers? How Germany Avoids Britain's Supply-Side Bottleneck.* London: Anglo-German Foundation.

Rowe, Vivian, 1959. *The Great Wall of France.* London: Putnam.

Schumpeter, Joseph A., 1946. 'The American Economy in the Interwar Years', *American Economic Review*, 36, supp., 1–10.

Scott, James C., 1985. *Weapons of the Weak: Everyday Forms of Peasant Resistance.* New Haven: Yale University Press.

Simon, Herbert A., 1969. *The Sciences of the Artificial.* Cambridge, MA: MIT Press.

Simon, Herbert A., 1978. 'Rationality as Process and as Product of Thought', *American Economic Review*, 68, 2, 1–16.

Simon, Herbert A., 1979. 'Rational Decision Making in Business Organizations', *American Economic Review*, 69, 4, 493–513.

Stone, Randall W., 2002. *Lending Credibility: The International Monetary Fund and the Post-Communist Tradition.* Princeton: Princeton University Press.

Studlar, Donley, 2004. 'Tobacco Control Policy Instruments in a Shrinking World: How Much Policy Learning?' In E. Vigoda and D. Levi-Faur, eds., *Policy Learning and Policy Beyond Regional, Cultural and Political Boundaries.* New York: Marcel Dekker.

Teague, Paul, 2002. 'Standard-Setting for Labour in Regional Trading Blocs: The EU and NAFTA Compared', *Journal of Public Policy*, 22, 3, 325–348.

Thompson, George, 1961. *The Inspiration of Science.* London: Oxford University Press.

Tocqueville, Alexis de, 1954. *Democracy in America.* New York: Vintage Books, 2 volumes.

Truman, Harry S, 1956. *Memoirs: Years of Trial and Hope.* Garden City, NY: Doubleday & Co., volume 2.

Turner, Barry, ed., 2002. *The Statesman's Yearbook 2002: The Politics, Cultures and Economics of the World.* Basingstoke: Palgrave Macmillan.

United Nations, Department of Public Economics and Public Administration, 2003. *Benchmarking E-Government: A Global Perspective.* New York: United Nations.

Walker, Robert and Wiseman, Michael, eds., 2003. *The Welfare We Want? The British Challenge for American Reform*. Bristol: The Policy Press.

Watson, Alan, 1976. 'Legal Transplants and Law Reform', *Law Quarterly Review*, 79, 79–109.

Watson, James L., ed., 1997. *Golden Arches East: McDonald's in East Asia*. Stanford: Stanford University Press.

Wenger, Etienne, 1998. *Communities of Practice: Learning, Meaning and Identity*. Cambridge: Cambridge University Press.

Westney, Eleanor, 1987. *Innovation and Imitation: The Transformation of Western Organizational Patterns to Meiji Japan*. Cambridge, MA: Harvard University Press.

Wilson, Graham K., 1998. *Only in America? The Politics of the United States in Comparative Perspective*. Chatham, NJ: Chatham House.

Wolman, Harold and Page, Edward C., 2000. *Learning from the Experience of Others: Policy Transfer among Local Regeneration Partnerships*. York: Joseph Rowntree Foundation.

World Bank, 2002a. *Building Institutions for Markets: World Development Report*. Washington, DC: World Bank.

World Bank, 2002b. *Transition: The First Ten Years. Analysis and Lessons for Eastern Europe and the Former Soviet Union*. Washington, DC: World Bank.

World Bank, 2002c. *World Bank Atlas 2002*. Washington, DC: World Bank.

Index